ARCHEOLOGY IN THE ADIRONDACKS

ARCHEOLOGY IN THE ADIRONDACKS

THE LAST FRONTIER

David R. Starbuck

UNIVERSITY PRESS OF NEW ENGLAND | HANOVER AND LONDON

University Press of New England

© 2018 University Press of New England

All rights reserved

Manufactured in the United States of America

Designed by April Leidig

Typeset in Whitman by Copperline Book Services, Inc.

For permission to reproduce any of the material in this book, contact
Brandeis University Press, 415 South Street, Waltham, MA 02453,
or visit brandeisuniversitypress.com

Library of Congress Cataloging-in-Publication Data

Name: Starbuck, David R., author.

Title: Archeology in the Adirondacks : the last frontier / David R. Starbuck.

Description: Hanover : University Press of New England, 2018 | Includes
    bibliographical references and index. |

Identifiers: LCCN 2017053905 (print) | LCCN 2017061745 (ebook) |
    ISBN 9781512602630 (epub, mobi, & pdf) | ISBN 9781512602623
    (pbk. : alk. paper) | ISBN 9781512602630 (ebook)

Subjects: LCSH: Adirondack Mountains Region (N.Y.) — Antiquities. |
    Excavations (Archaeology) — New York (State) — Adirondack Mountains
    Region. | Archaeology and history — New York (State) — Adirondack
    Mountains Region.

Classification: LCC F127.A2 (ebook) | LCC F127.A2 S638 2018 (print) |
    DDC 974.7 — dc23

LC record available at https://lccn.loc.gov/2017053905

5 4 3

CONTENTS

PREFACE

My ancestors first came to live in the Adirondack Mountains in the late 1700s. I was raised on a farm in Chestertown, a small village in the southeast corner of what is now the Adirondack Park. While I was growing up there in the 1950s and '60s, eagerly planning to become an archeologist, my parents and others warned me that I would have to pursue my career elsewhere, as there were no archeological sites in the Adirondacks. "All the best sites" were supposed to be far away and far back in time. How could the Adirondacks possibly compete with the ruins of early civilizations or pueblos or prehistoric mounds? My response, like that of so many other young people, was to leave the mountains, and my career carried me to excavations in Mexico and to archeological digs that I have directed throughout New York, New England, and Scotland.

I am writing this to make the point that the time periods and sites we archeologists study are now very different. Fifty years ago, American archeologists chiefly studied Native Americans and other "early" cultures, and there was a popular misconception that few Native American sites existed in the Adirondacks. No one wanted to believe that anyone lived in mountainous areas before the nineteenth century, and the same was said for the Green Mountains and the White Mountains just to the east. Also, when I was a boy, the more recent historical sites or industrial sites were seldom thought of as being worthy of archeology, and I doubted that archeologists would ever take an interest in such places. People saw no point in duplicating what was already known through historical sources.

All that has changed, of course. Here in the Adirondacks we have Native American camp sites and fishing sites, early dugout canoes, logging camps, incredible mining sites, abandoned farms and ghost towns, "lost" ski areas, abandoned fire towers, and much, much more. Today we believe that *all* these sites have value and that traditional history tells no more than a small fraction of the story about people and how they have occupied and modified the Adirondack landscape. Archeology, by relying on physical remains, tells the stories of ordinary people, not just those who were wealthy and prominent and for whom there is already a written record. Instead of studying just the largely absentee owners of the Great Camps in the Adirondacks, we have become curious about the year-round residents, the loggers, the farmers, the miners, and even the working-class women who seasonally came to Wiawaka Holiday House on Lake George to get a vacation from their factory jobs in Troy and Cohoes.

This book is titled "Archeology *in* the Adirondacks," rather than "*of* the Adirondacks," because it is not possible to cover all the thousands of archeological sites throughout the Adirondack Park. Instead, I have selected a modest sampling of representative sites, especially on the eastern side of the park, that give a feeling for the very special cultural resources that are present in northern New York State. There are truly great sites and ruins throughout the Adirondacks, and this volume gives me a chance to demonstrate that every archeologist is a storyteller. I want to tell some stories about the archeology that has been conducted in the Adirondacks and about the many cultural "survivals" in our region.

In order to do this, I have received help from a great many people in preparing this book. First, I wish to thank Phyllis Deutsch, acquisitions editor at the University Press of New England, who patiently nudged me along as I completed the manuscript that became this book. Phyllis has worked with me on several previous books, and her encouragement has always been essential to developing the right "tone" for each volume. Next, I wish to thank all the archeologists, both avocational and professional—they are too numerous to list here—who have worked with me on some of the projects described in this book. But I especially wish to mention Linda White and Paula Dennis, who participated on digs at my farm; George and Peg Wertime, Linda Culver, Cheryl Walker, Betty Hall, Naomi Bedell, Brad Jarvis, and Sarah Waite, who dug with me at the Chester Inn; Carolyn Weatherwax, who has been extremely informative about graphite mining; and every last archeologist who worked with me at Fort William Henry and the Lake George Battlefield Park—there have been at least a few hundred of these field and laboratory workers, thanks to the annual sponsorship of these digs by SUNY Adirondack. Many of these workers have also been members of the Adirondack Chapter of the New York State Archaeological Association, which has been another generous sponsor of this research. I also wish to thank Sarah Majot, owner of the archeological contract firm ARCH TECH (based in Albany), for many observations about Adirondack sites and for advice on illustrations to include in this volume.

While I personally prepared most of the photographs that appear here, I owe an enormous thanks to Tom Weinman, who provided several of the most interesting illustrations in chapter 2 (from the Weinman site on Lake George).

I have received very necessary interest and support from Kathy Muncil, Melodie Viele, Pam and Steve Collyer, and Bruce Nelson, all at Fort William Henry; Charles Vandrei, historic preservation officer for the New York State Department of Environmental Conservation; Christina Rieth, Michael Lucas,

Andrea Lain, Susan Winchell-Sweeney, and Kristin O'Connell at the New York State Museum; Lyn Hohmann, president of the Fort George Alliance; Bruce and Suzanne Robbins, owners of the Chester Inn; Dan Smith of Horicon, who guided me to sites in the town of Graphite; John O'Donnell, caretaker for Pack Demonstration Forest, who showed me fireplaces, mines, and kilns in the forest; and Jim Speenburgh, Marty Cooper, Billy MacGlashan, John Shafer, and Andy LeBlanc, all of whom helped by saving artifacts as they worked at the Starbuck Farm.

Finally, several of these chapters, now expanded and updated, originated as articles in the magazine *Adirondack Life*. I would especially like to thank Niki Kourofsky and Elizabeth Folwell for allowing me to use some of that material as the core of chapters 3, 5, 6, and 7. *Adirondack Life* has always been my favorite magazine because it tells stories about the people who make the Adirondack Mountains a very special place.

David R. Starbuck
June 2017

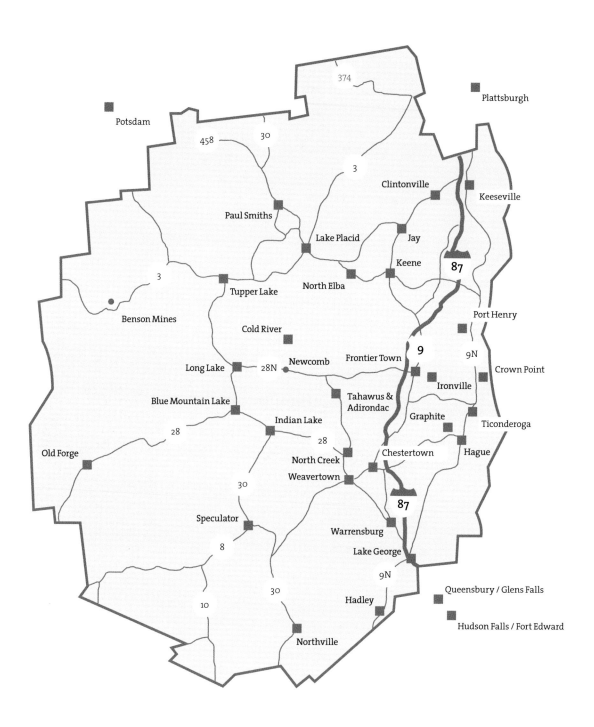

Potsdam

374

Plattsburgh

458   30

3

Clintonville

Keeseville

Paul Smiths

Lake Placid   Jay

Keene

87

3

Tupper Lake   North Elba

Benson Mines

Cold River

Port Henry

Long Lake   28N   Newcomb   Frontier Town   9   9N

Crown Point

Blue Mountain Lake

Tahawus &
Adirondac

Ironville

Graphite

Ticonderoga

28

28

Old Forge

North Creek   Chestertown   Hague

Indian Lake

Weavertown

30   87

Speculator

Warrensburg

8

Lake George

9N

30

Hadley

Queensbury / Glens Falls

10

Northville

Hudson Falls / Fort Edward

ARCHEOLOGY IN THE ADIRONDACKS

1.1.
A view from the edge of my
farm, looking north into the
Adirondack Mountains.

TRACES OF THE PAST IN THE ADIRONDACKS

ONE

The Adirondack Mountains are one of the greatest natural wonders in the eastern United States. Blessed with abundant mineral resources, woodlands, lakes, rivers, and spectacular natural vistas just about everywhere, the Adirondacks have welcomed visitors for thousands of years (fig. 1.1). For their part, both residents and visitors have left behind a great many historical and archeological sites that scholars have studied for only the past forty to fifty years (Folwell 1992; Masten 1968; Tyler and Wilson 2009; Williams 2002). Today, archeologists, historians, hikers, and cross-country skiers are able to enjoy viewing the remains of past life in the Adirondacks, with many of the ruins largely undisturbed.

Given the size of the Adirondack region, archeology has only lightly sampled its traces of the past. (The Adirondack Park is defined as being within "the blue line," an area of 3,125 square miles, or about 6.1 million acres.) Professors and their students from colleges on the fringes of the Adirondack Park arrive in the summers to carry out archeological research, perhaps following much the same routes as the Native Americans who entered the Adirondacks seasonally to hunt and fish. In a seasonally recurring pattern, it seems only natural that college field schools would come here for a few months each summer to give students hands-on experience in archeology, and then we all go home again (or back to school) in the fall. Most modern vacationers follow the same pattern, arriving seasonally to occupy summer camps or wintertime ski areas in the Adirondacks.

In my own case, I have been fortunate to be involved in archeological field-work in New York State since 1970, and I have directed excavations since 1991 at the southeastern corner of the park through the auspices of the State University of New York (SUNY) Adirondack, formerly Adirondack Community College. Far to the north, SUNY Plattsburgh has worked on industrial sites and cellar holes at the northeastern corner of the Adirondacks for many years, thanks to the efforts of Drs. Gordon Pollard, James Dawson, and their colleagues. On the western side of the Adirondack Park, faculty based at SUNY Potsdam have worked on both historic and prehistoric sites in the Adirondacks for even longer. There is no direct collaboration among these disparate schools, but clearly we all recognize that the Adirondacks offer very special historic and prehistoric resources that provide solid learning experiences for our students.

Given the modest scale of many of these research projects, it may require an institution more centrally based within the Adirondack Park to generate a year-round program of field investigations. Archeology has great potential here, because the seasonal nature of many activities in the Adirondacks resulted in residents often "walking away" from their camps, ski areas, industries, and logging operations, such that the woods are now relatively full of abandoned huts, camps, mines, and equipment (Bramen 2016). An immense number of cultural survivals remain within the Adirondack Park, awaiting hands-on documentation by scholars today and those of generations to come.

What Can We Hope to Find?

Among the many historical sites in the Adirondacks offering excellent research potential are the abandoned towns, popularly referred to as ghost towns. Best-known among these is the community of Adirondac, first occupied by a mining community between 1826 and 1858, later by cottages used as hunting lodges (1876–1947), and then by mine workers while titanium mining was going on nearby (Manchester 2007; Verner 1968). The community was abandoned for good in 1963. I remember visiting here with my Boy Scout troop while I was in the seventh grade, as we were about to ascend Mount Marcy, and I recall that the buildings were still standing but no longer occupied. Today most of the houses have collapsed (fig. 1.2), and the only building that has been preserved is the MacNaughton cottage where Vice President Theodore Roosevelt and his family were staying in 1901 when they received word that President McKinley had been shot (Esch 2012) (fig. 1.3).

Perhaps not as well known, but just as interesting in its own way, is the community of Graphite (fig. 1.4), which has a great many cellar holes, as well as industrial ruins. The settlement of Graphite was the largest of several small communities in the eastern Adirondacks that grew up around the mining of graphite in the late 1800s; these hamlets stretch from the town of Wilton in the south for a distance of about sixty miles north to Ticonderoga. A crushing mill, boardinghouses, sheds, sawmills, and other specialized buildings were all necessary to support the mining operations around Graphite. When cheaper labor and other sources of the mineral elsewhere brought mining operations to a halt in 1921, salvage activities soon removed the buildings and machinery, and the forest quickly obscured the foundations that were left. This pattern has been repeated hundreds of times over in the Adirondacks, with extractive industries lasting only as long as easily accessible veins of ore and low-priced labor were available.

1.2. ▲
The ruins of one of the houses at Adirondac in June 2017. Of the many crumbling dwellings at this abandoned ghost town, this one has the most intact fireplace and chimney.

1.3. ▶
The MacNaughton cottage in the community of Adirondac in June 2017. As noted on the interpretive panel, this "is the only wood frame structure that remains from the iron mining era." Facing collapse, it was acquired and restored by the Open Space Institute.

1.4.
Historical plaque
for the abandoned
town of Graphite.

Also of note are abandoned camps of the public works program known as the Civilian Conservation Corps (CCC). Eleven of these camps were constructed in the Adirondacks, to provide work for unemployed men during the Great Depression, and between 1933 and 1942 they built roads, camps, trails, dams, fire towers, and more, and nationwide they planted nearly three billion trees (Podskoch 2011; Hodges 2016). One of the best of the Adirondack camps is in Pack Demonstration Forest in Warrensburg, where the ruins of mess halls and abandoned mines (both lime and graphite) are attractively dispersed throughout the forest (fig. 1.5). My father worked as a foreman for the CCC (at a different camp), and he recounted fond memories every time we drove past the turnoff on Route 9 for Pack Forest. Across the country some 2.5 million young men worked for the CCC, and the ruins of their Adirondack camps should provide wonderful fodder for archeologists and labor historians.

There also are small, nearly abandoned hamlets and crossroads almost everywhere in the Adirondacks, many of which would be ideal candidates for archeological research. As an example, a recent publication featured a hamlet that is very close to me:

Starbuckville: In 1846, Isaac Starbuck started a tannery along the Schroon River in the area now known as Starbuckville. Starbuckville grew into a thriving community. In addition to the tannery, there were several mills, including a carding mill and a grist mill all operating in and around the mill dam. The Sunnyside Hotel was built in the late 1870s on the south

1.5.

The surviving fireplace and chimney from a ccc mess hall in Pack Forest. ccc Camp
S-101, Company 289, established its camp here on May 17, 1934; about two hundred men
lived in tents and worked on forestry projects in 1934–1935. The camp was closed on
January 9, 1936.

side of the bridge by Edgar Bentley. There was also a school district & several boarding houses for tannery workers. A shoe manufacturing business, started by Isaac Starbuck and his brothers Edward and George, burned down in 1870. The Sunnyside Hotel was destroyed by fire in 1905. The other remaining buildings have either burned, fallen down or been remodeled. (*Adirondack Journal*, June 8, 2013, 10)

I clearly have a personal interest in Starbuckville, which is only two miles from my home in Chestertown; in fact, Isaac Starbuck grew up in the farmhouse that I now occupy. Sadly, the type of abandonment that occurred in Starbuckville is all too frequent throughout the Adirondacks, with highly mobile populations often seeking higher wages or cultural amenities farther west or closer to major population centers (fig. 1.6).

Of course, structures in the built environment that are rapidly becoming archeological sites do not have to be the size of a town or even a hamlet. There are some thirty-two steel observation (fire) towers scattered throughout the Adirondacks, and one tower has become an outdoor exhibit at the Adirondack Experience, the Museum on Blue Mountain Lake, formerly the Adirondack Museum (fig. 1.7). Given the changing methods for detecting fires, these

1.6.
Abandoned house in the hamlet of Starbuckville, a community that has shrunk greatly since the 1800s.

1.7.
The Whiteface Mountain Observation Tower, built in 1919 and now on display at the Adirondack Experience, the Museum on Blue Mountain Lake.

towers are no longer used to spot fires in the park and now are simply beautiful "relics" on the summits of mountains (Stoltie 2016).

Another interesting cultural feature in the park, on a much smaller scale, are the many dugout canoes that traveled local waterways; several of these dugouts have been discovered submerged in shallow ponds. Dugouts continued to be used into the early historic period, so it is sometimes unclear whether a particular example is Native American or whether it might have been used by European hunters, fishermen, and trappers in the eighteenth and nineteenth centuries. The current authority on this topic is Curt Stager, a professor of natural sciences at Paul Smith's College, a four-year institution that is roughly centered within the Adirondack Park. Stager has taken wood samples from several of these canoes for radiocarbon dating. One such dugout (fig. 1.8) was found in Daggett Pond in Warren County, just west of Pack Forest, and "is most likely between about 200 and 350 years old" (Stager, personal communication, Sept. 3, 2014). Like many other dugouts, it shows signs of metal tool use on the wood, which does not necessarily mean it was created by European craftsmen, since Native Americans used steel tools during the early historic period.

"So far, all but the Twin Ponds dugouts have had similar metal tool marks on them and lack of extensive charring, meaning 3–3.5 centuries or less in age," Stager says. "This makes sense, as they came from shallow water; lake levels before that time period were much lower, so the older boats are probably farther out from shore now and also covered by more lake mud."

These are but a few examples of the many types of cultural features in or on the landscape that are in the process of becoming archeological sites. Clearly, sites in the Adirondacks do not have to be very old, as long as they exemplify the distinctiveness and character of this region. Even plane crash sites are now thought of as archeological sites. Forest ranger Scott van Laer has been referred to as an "aviation archaeologist," as he studies the remains of dozens of planes that have gone down in the Adirondack Mountains (Esch 2016).

Like the plane crashes and CCC camps, sites dating from the twentieth century hold their own interest. There were excavations in 2013 and 2014 at Wiawaka Holiday House at the southern end of Lake George (fig. 1.9). Wiawaka was formed in 1903 as a vacation retreat for young female textile workers from Troy and Cohoes. In the early years it provided a peaceful getaway for women who otherwise could not have been able to afford a vacation on Lake George; the activities at Wiawaka were organized by retreat managers. "These types of vacation spots [holiday houses] were set up by upper and middle class women through churches and private organizations, as well as by labor unions and some companies" (Toscano 2013, A6).

1.8.
A dugout canoe found in Daggett Pond, being wheeled out of storage at Fort William Henry. Hand-hewn from a tree trunk, it is now on display in the Rogers Island Visitors Center in Fort Edward. It measures 18 feet, 5 inches long and has a maximum width of 2 feet. Made of cedar, it was donated by Melvin W. Hathaway to Fort William Henry in 1967.

1.9.
The signboard at the entrance to Wiawaka Holiday House in Lake George.

A great many women have vacationed at Wiawaka since then, coming from many different backgrounds, and archeology has now been used to recover trash from dumps on the property. The recent work was directed by Megan Springate, a doctoral candidate at the University of Maryland, supervising more than a dozen volunteers from ages eighteen to seventy-five.

A central question for Springate and her colleagues was whether the garbage from a 1920s' dump could demonstrate what might have been appropriate behavior for working-class women who visited Wiawaka during those years. Did they wear makeup? Did they wear the same things that middle-class women liked to wear at that time? Put another way, would white, middle-class standards of femininity determine what was in the dump? (Working-class women could have been viewed as somewhat wanton if they wore too much lipstick or other makeup.) Among the archeologists' many finds was Pond's Cream, a moisturizer used "to preserve the whiteness of the skin," but there was no lipstick in the dump. Springate has presented this study as an example of "feminist archeology," perhaps the very first to be conducted in the Adirondacks. The stories of working-class women have rarely been told through archeology, so this is clearly a significant and rare study when placed in a rural setting.

The work at Wiawaka, a retreat for white, Christian women, naturally prompts the question, "What other groups in the Adirondacks deserve special attention?" Can we show ethnic diversity in the Adirondack Mountains? Ethnicity studies is a popular theme in modern archeology, and we must ask whether archeology can be used to identify distinctive remains from the descendants of British, African, French, and other early settlers, and also of Native Americans living here during the historic period. What might you find at an Anglo homestead versus a French homestead, or at one of the logging camps, or a hunting camp, and so on? The dig at Timbuctoo, an African American settlement (described in chapter 5) explores the adaptation of African Americans to farming life in the Adirondacks. Every one of these ethnic settlements might be expected to have rather different artifact types, but that can be proven only through systematic fieldwork conducted at multiple sites.

Another type of site with very special significance would be the many underground railroad sites where runaway slaves were sheltered while en route to Canada. What artifacts could you hope to find that would indicate the presence of the underground railroad or African Americans? After all, primary documents mentioning the sheltering of runaway slaves are rare, since the hiding or transport of runaways was illegal. Could archeology find evidence that is not in the written record? A very systematic treatment of this subject is presented in the North Star Underground Railroad Museum in Keeseville (fig. 1.10). This fascinating museum with its very dedicated staff has a leg iron on display; its exhibit label states that it was "discovered by John Lecky in 1970 during renovation of the former home of Pliny Hoag on Hallock Hill, Town of Ausable. It had been hidden under floor boards at the top of a stairway leading to the attic" (fig. 1.11).

Turning in a very different direction, modern archeology often delights in revealing the seamier side of life, especially by examining what are popularly termed "houses of ill repute." Past excavations in urban areas have often shown

1.10. ▲
The North Star Underground Railroad Museum in Keeseville.

1.11. ◄
A leg iron on display, perhaps removed from the leg of a runaway slave. This is the type of evidence for the Underground Railroad that archeologists hope to find.

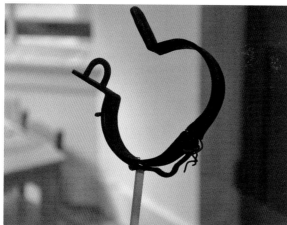

that employees of these establishments lived surprisingly well, with furnishings meant to attract and entertain high-paying clientele. The privy holes behind brothels often contain the most fascinating range of trash, objects never meant to be seen by "proper" society (fig. 1.12). While such contexts have been explored in the Five Points neighborhood of New York City and elsewhere (Yamin et al. 2000), what might we hope to find in more rural areas such as the Adirondacks? I have been making inquiries about the locations of some of these colorful sites for years, and future archeologists working in the Adirondacks will hopefully have the chance to explore some brothels.

1.12.
A rustic privy house on display at the Adirondack Experience, the Museum on Blue Mountain Lake. Covered in spruce bark and originally built in 1906, this privy stood in a camp on the western shore of Long Lake before it was moved to the museum.

Another category of site not yet examined archeologically in the Adirondacks would be the houses and barns that sheltered vehicles engaged in rum-running and other illegal activities during the Prohibition era of the 1920s. My father often described witnessing the "barn on Stock Farm Road" (in Warrensburg) where vehicles would come out only at night, ready to race to the Canadian border and then back with their cargoes of alcohol. Can we hope to find artifacts from Prohibition-era dumps, liquor bottles, stills, or even some of the automobiles, showing us how Adirondackers defied the law during this colorful time in our history?

Telling the Story of the Adirondacks

While it would be satisfying for readers to visit the countless prehistoric and historic sites across this region, it might be more practical to begin with a visit to the Adirondack Experience on Blue Mountain Lake (fig. 1.13). Since 1957, this museum has been the historical lifeblood of the Adirondack region, and many of us proudly claim that the museum tells the story of "our" respective families.

1.13.
The Visitor Center at the entrance to the Adirondack Experience in May 2017.

To this may be added the many fine exhibits at the Lake George Historical Association, Crown Point State Historic Site, Fort Ticonderoga, Fort William Henry, the Adirondack Iron and Steel Company in Tahawus, the Penfield Homestead Museum in Ironville, the Clinton County Historical Museum in Plattsburgh, the North Star Underground Railroad Museum in Keeseville, the Goodsell Museum in Old Forge, and Great Camp Sagamore in Raquette Lake. All these attractions are listed in the appendix, with information on how to contact each site. Every one of these historic sites and museums has a story about the Adirondacks that is worth telling. Also, the Wild Center in Tupper Lake, while a natural history museum, is currently the most-visited educational center in the Adirondack Park.

Beyond the interpretive sites found within the Adirondack Park, a short drive outside the park will take the visitor to the Six Nations Indian Museum in Onchiota (just northwest of the park); the Iroquois Indian Museum in Howes Cave; the New York State Museum in Albany; the Slate Valley Museum in Granville; the Fort House Museum and the Rogers Island Visitors Center in Fort Edward; and the Skenesborough Museum in Whitehall. Through powerful and people-friendly exhibits, area museums present wonderful and inspirational stories about all of those who have called the Adirondacks home over the years.

2.1.

Postcard of "Indian Basket Makers" in the Adirondacks. On the back it reads: "One of the picturesque features of life in that great American playground, the Adirondacks, is found in the presence, in all parts of the woods, of parties of Indian basket makers. These Indians live in either tents or rustic lodges and spend their time in making fancy baskets and bead work, which they sell to the tourists. All the members of a family of Indians thus employed, even to children of six or eight years, take an active part in the basket making."

TWO

Tom Weinman likes to tell the story of how he received a phone call from his father in 1964, describing his parents' discovery of some Indian pottery on their property at Assembly Point, a peninsula near the southern end of Lake George. Tom jumped into his car and drove to their camp in less than an hour. The wonderful result for Tom has been fifty years as an avocational archeologist who explores Native American sites, enjoying the sheer thrill of discovery alongside the most-visited lake in the Adirondacks.

For thousands of years, Lake George has welcomed Native Americans who truly love the beauty of this region (figs. 2.1 and 2.2). As we look north and west from that lake into the heart of the Adirondacks, we are reminded of the conventional belief that Native Americans would not have wanted to live in mountainous areas; that the growing season would have been too brief and that natural resources would not have been rich enough to support year-round settlements. These popular opinions have oftentimes caused archeologists to avoid uplands and to focus instead on the sides of rivers and lakes in lower, more temperate zones. That is unfortunate, because archeological surveys in the Adirondacks, especially along waterways on the eastern side of the mountains, are increasingly providing evidence for large, albeit seasonal, occupations. While Native American settlements may oftentimes have been brief throughout the Adirondacks, Lake George was clearly a superb area for fishing and hunting, and it would always have been a popular destination during the warmer months of the year.

The Native American presence lasted well into the historic period, as disparate cultures either fought or traded with each other. Skilled makers of handicrafts were frequent summertime visitors from Canada in the nineteenth and early twentieth centuries. Even today, Native Americans continue to be a very important part of this region, and the prehistoric and historic sites they have created will no doubt become an ever more popular focus for scholars.

The first European visitors to the Adirondacks, whether they were soldiers, traders, or trappers, generally camped in the same areas, for the same reasons, as the Native Americans who had foraged here since the end of the Pleistocene (the late Wisconsin period). The time of first entry into this region after the retreat of glacial ice was sometime between 11,500 and 13,000 years ago, with archeologists often in disagreement about the dating of the very earliest sites.

2.2.
A view of Lake George, facing northeast. Courtesy of Tom and Paul Weinman.

The first Paleo-Indian hunter-gatherers, organized in small bands, moved seasonally through the major river valleys, relying on an extremely diversified diet that included everything from wild plant foods to Pleistocene megafauna. An elevated bluff with a superb view, easy access to waterways that provided fish and good transportation, well-drained soil where you could erect a shelter — these are a few of the factors that helped to determine where native peoples would create their campsites. They also help archeologists to predict where traces of those campsites might have survived down to the present day. Many of the Adirondack sites were very short term, occupied for only a night or two, and yet a few flakes of stone, some staining, or a potsherd can help professional archeologists to tell a story.

Who were the first residents of the Adirondacks? Where are their descendants today? Why don't we hear more about them? Scholars point out that during early historic times, portions of this region were occupied by Mohicans (Mahicans) coming from the south along the Hudson River (Dunn 1994), as well as Mohawks coming from the west and southwest (Snow 1996), and Abenakis coming from the east and from the Lake Champlain area (Wiseman 2001). Each of these peoples has contributed greatly to the blending of cultures that we find in the Adirondacks today, and fortunately there are many places where the public may go to learn more about them.

2.3.
The opening panel of a basketry exhibit at the Adirondack Experience.

The many visitors to the New York State Museum in Albany are able to enjoy archeological and ethnographic exhibits and collections that present the interpretations of professional archeologists and museum curators, even though most exhibits deal with the more heavily populated, more southerly regions of the state. There are also excellent exhibits and collections at the Rochester Museum of Science, the Iroquois Indian Museum at Howes Cave, the new Seneca-Iroquois National Museum in Salamanca, and at other museums as well. And just northwest of the Adirondacks, the Six Nations Indian Museum in Onchiota, founded in 1954 by Ray Fadden and now directed by John Fadden and his sons Don and Dave, is an absolutely essential place to visit. There also are attractive ethnographic exhibits at the Adirondack Experience on Blue Mountain Lake (fig. 2.3) and prehistoric and ethnographic exhibits at the Lake George Historical Association, the Clinton County Historical Museum in Plattsburgh, Fort William Henry, and Fort Ticonderoga.

In addition, the Conference on Iroquois Research holds annual conventions at various locations throughout the state, with presentations of fresh research; together with many annual powwows throughout the region and meetings hosted by the New York State Archaeological Association, there are ample ways to learn about the strong Native American presence in New York State.

Chronology

Archeologists working throughout New York State and the Northeast have established time periods for the development of early cultures in the region, relying on hundreds of excavations and numerous radiocarbon (carbon 14) dates. However, even William Ritchie, the New York State archaeologist who personally formulated the essential chronologies for much of the Northeast (Ritchie 1969), conducted very little fieldwork in the Adirondacks.

Artifact typologies have been developed that make it possible to place even random finds into fairly tight time brackets. Site files maintained by the New York State Office of Parks, Recreation and Historic Preservation, and by the New York State Museum, with restricted access, document the locations of numerous known sites throughout the Adirondacks. It thus is possible to develop predictive models for where other sites might be located, given the proximity of natural resources and other, already known sites. By relying upon radiocarbon dating, these sites are typically assigned to one or more of the following time periods, which reflect an ever-increasing technological and artistic sophistication, as well as increasing sedentism:

> Paleo-Indian (ca. 11000–8000 BC)
> Early Archaic (ca. 8000–6000 BC)
> Middle Archaic (ca. 6000–4000 BC)
> Late Archaic (ca. 4000–1800 BC)
> Terminal Archaic (ca. 1800–1000 BC)
> Early Woodland (ca. 1000–100 BC)
> Middle Woodland (ca. 100 BC–AD 1000)
> Late Woodland (ca. AD 1000–1500)

Paleo-Indian hunter-gatherers were followed by more diversified Archaic cultures that relied on hunting, fishing, collecting shellfish, and gathering of wild plant foods. As modern floral and faunal species appeared, the population density grew, and mixed deciduous forests allowed for higher carrying capacities and more of a "settling in" effect along small lakes and streams. By the Woodland period, pottery appeared along with burial ceremonialism and, finally, some horticulture after about AD 700 (Hart and Rieth 2002).

With the entry of Europeans into the region, this sequence ends with what we term the Contact period, after which the written historical record provides additional information about the presence of native peoples in the Adirondacks (Sulavik 2005). Thus our knowledge of Native Americans' life in the region after this date derives from a combination of oral history, written history, and archeological findings, and these three approaches are equally important for achieving a better understanding of the history and traditions of native peoples. However, a great many Native Americans were displaced after the wars of the eighteenth century, and cultural survival sometimes meant maintaining a very low visibility down to the present day.

Archeological Fieldwork

The first systematic inventory of archeological sites in the Adirondacks was included within Arthur Parker's *The Archeological History of New York* (1922), which listed all known prehistoric sites (as of the 1920s) by county. Every county within the Adirondacks was represented, although generally with only six to ten known sites per county. Those figures appear incredibly low today, and work by both professional and avocational archeologists — oftentimes during the course of cultural resource management surveys — has located a great many additional sites. As early as 1985, Hartgen Archeological Associates was able to prepare an inventory of over 350 known prehistoric and industrial sites in the Adirondacks, and the total number of identified sites is easily several times higher today. Other syntheses of prehistoric sites include *The Original People: Native Americans in the Champlain Valley* (1988) and *Native American Presence, Lake George* (Adamson 2017). Also, excellent overviews of Native American cultures in the Adirondacks have been published in *Adirondack Life* magazine by Lynn Woods (1994) and Curt Stager (2017), both of whom have synthesized archeological findings with information from interviews conducted with Native Americans and artifact collectors.

Fieldwork at prehistoric sites in the Adirondacks has often focused on the peripheries where colleges have conducted excavations, but far and away the most intensive work has been conducted on the sides of Lake George, where William Ritchie undertook limited excavations on the grounds of Fort William Henry in the 1950s, followed by Robert Funk at several sites in the 1960s. Funk's collaboration with Tom and Paul Weinman at the Weinman site on Assembly Point (Funk 1976) stands out especially (figs. 2.4 and 2.5).

As already mentioned, this was Tom Weinman's very first dig, as they rolled the sod back, dug in five-foot squares, and observed how the artifact types changed as they went deeper (Weinman 2017). At shallower depths, they found much Middle Woodland pottery with cord marking; projectile points (spear points and arrowheads) of the Levanna, Fox Creek, and Jack's Reef Corner-Notched types (fig. 2.6); and assorted drills, net sinkers, a drilled gorget, end scrapers, and large bifaces (two-faced stone tools). The stone tools were made of Normanskill chert and Fort Ann chert, with lesser quantities of quartz and quartzite. Bone did not preserve here because of the acid soil. A very significant find was a large roasting platform made of fire-cracked rocks, presumably for processing fish (fig. 2.7).

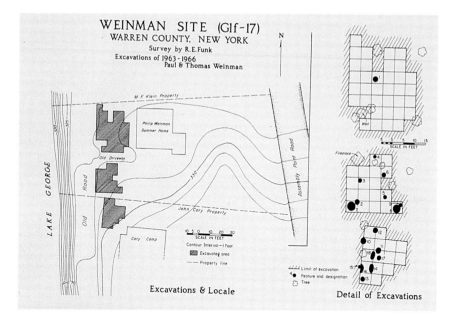

2.4.
Plan view of areas
excavated at the
Weinman site on
Assembly Point.
Courtesy of Tom and
Paul Weinman.

2.5.
Dr. Robert Funk at
the Weinman site.
Courtesy of Tom and
Paul Weinman.

As they went deeper, the Weinmans and Funk found larger numbers of stemmed projectile points, bifaces, gouges, and a pestle. Continuing still farther down, they found Vosburg and Brewerton projectile points. Then, at the very bottom, they found Otter Creek projectile points and a ground-slate ulu, or flat-bladed knife (fig. 2.8). The stratigraphy here was amazing, as each occupation or settlement could be distinguished from the next, and while it had not

2.6. ▲◄
Lithic tools from the Weinman site, shallower levels. Courtesy of Tom and Paul Weinman.

2.7. ▲
Roasting platform of fire-cracked rocks discovered at the Weinman site. Courtesy of Tom and Paul Weinman.

2.8. ◄
Lithic tools from the Weinman site, lower levels. Courtesy of Tom and Paul Weinman.

been possible to obtain any radiocarbon dates at this site, the changing artifact typologies revealed occupations dating as far back as 4500 BC.

This had been some of the earliest and most productive prehistoric archeology in the Adirondacks, and at just one site, the Weinmans and Funk had uncovered occupations from the Late Archaic period through the late Middle Woodland period (Funk 1976). Since they then proceeded to find and explore other sites along the shores of Lake George, it may be argued that no other fieldwork in the Adirondacks has ever been as enlightening, and they

2.9.
A view of Long Lake in 2017. The lake was a popular hunting and fishing destination for Native Americans.

successfully demonstrated that Lake George has the richest known Native American sites in the region.

In the late 1970s, new fieldwork was conducted a few miles away by Dean Snow (then a professor at SUNY Albany) at the Harrisena site, where Snow found an Early Archaic assemblage of bifurcate-base projectile points, Plano and Kirk points, knives, and scrapers, most of which had been manufactured from quartz and quartzite (Snow 1977, 1980). Because of the high cost of basing a field team in Lake George during the summer tourist season, Snow's work was short-lived, but it had successfully pushed back knowledge of local native peoples by several thousand additional years.

In the years since then, Tom Weinman has discovered many more sites on Lake George, but Native American archeology in the interior of the Adirondacks has been fairly modest, except for surveys by Beth Wellman, Susan Winchell-Sweeney, and the New York State Museum. However, a new field project has begun on Long Lake (fig. 2.9) under the direction of Tim Messner and SUNY Potsdam, and rich artifact collections picked up along the shores of Long Lake for many years (Woods 1994) suggest that Messner will be able to successfully locate numerous prehistoric sites.

Returning our focus again to the Lake George area, we note that three quite large projects have been conducted around the lake in recent years.

THE GROUNDS OF FORT WILLIAM HENRY

The grounds of Fort William Henry contain some of the richest Native American features and artifacts ever found in the Adirondacks, and fieldwork there has been ongoing since the early 1950s. Stanley Gifford (fig. 2.10) exposed prehistoric hearths and artifacts everywhere he dug in the parade ground of the fort (Gifford 1955), and William Ritchie was called in at that time to excavate the remains of a Native American skeleton (Starbuck 2014, 13). Prehistoric artifacts recovered from the grounds of the fort in the 1950s included large numbers of projectile points from the Early Archaic through the Late Woodland periods, as well as lithic bifaces, scrapers, perforators, and worked flakes, plus very large numbers of pottery sherds. The number of bifurcate-base projectile points discovered at the fort was the largest ever found in the region, suggesting there may have been a significant population here in the Early Archaic (8000–6000 BC). The people who left these tools behind may well have been the distant ancestors of the Mohicans (or Mahicans) who during the early historic period occupied the waterways that lie between New York State and Vermont, from the southern end of Lake Champlain south to New York City and east into the Berkshires of Massachusetts (Dunn 1994).

My own work at the fort has been ongoing since 1997, conducted through SUNY Adirondack, and the college has located prehistoric sites that are almost as ubiquitous as the remains of soldiers and officers. Archeological evidence recovered at Fort William Henry thus suggests a pattern of thousands of years of occupation by native peoples prior to the arrival of French and British armies in the 1750s. During our recent work at the fort, we have found diagnostic

2.10.
Stanley Gifford measuring an ax head found at Fort William Henry in the 1950s. Courtesy of the Fort William Henry Corporation.

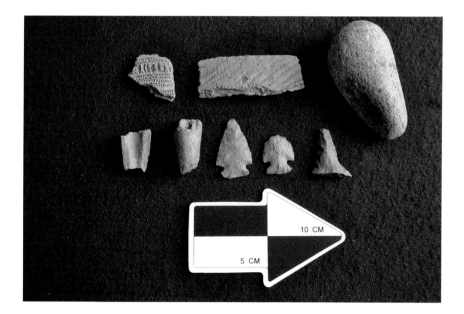

2.11.
Representative artifacts found in dumps outside the eastern wall of the reconstructed Fort William Henry.

stone tools inside the foundations of the West Barracks, the East Barracks, the north end of the parade ground, and in the dumps east of the fort (fig. 2.11) (Starbuck 2002b, 2014). We also uncovered two prehistoric fireplaces in 1997 that were still intact just underneath the surface of the parade ground, and we even found a single shell bead (wampum) in the cellar of the East Barracks in 2012. Pottery sherds are abundant, with most dating to the Middle Woodland period, as evidenced by much cord-impressed pottery, linear dentate decoration, some thumbnail decoration, and small circular punctate decoration.

Perhaps our most distinctive prehistoric discoveries have been two "roasting platforms," both found deeply buried outside the east wall of the fort. These platforms, where rocks were piled up for the processing (smoking or drying) of fish, are a type of feature typically found in the Middle Woodland period and located near rivers and other bodies of water. The platform we found in 1998 measured 2.1 by 1.6 meters (roughly 7 feet by 5 ¼ feet), and it has now been reconstructed and is on display inside the East Barracks of the fort (fig. 2.12). We found a second platform in 2012, only about 10 meters from the first; it measured 2 meters (6 ½ feet) east-west by a minimum of 1.27 meters (a little more than 4 feet) north-south, and it has been left where it was found (fig. 2.13).

Given the presence of at least two of these platforms on the grounds of the fort, it may be that the Middle Woodland was the richest period of occupation on the terrace where Fort William Henry was later constructed. Defining the full extent of these campsites should be an important goal during future excavations at the fort.

2.12. ◀
A large roasting platform of fire-cracked rocks found in 1998, now reconstructed inside Fort William Henry.

2.13. ▼
A second roasting platform found in 2012 outside the eastern wall of the reconstructed fort. This was subsequently reburied to protect it.

THE MILLION DOLLAR BEACH

Important excavations of Native American sites took place from the summer of 2013 until the spring of 2014 as the New York State Museum dug just south of what is popularly termed the "Million Dollar Beach" at the southern end of Lake George. A great many prehistoric sites are discovered purely by chance, and in this case New York State was planning to repave the beach parking lot and a stretch of Beach Road with a surface of porous pavement that would filter storm-water runoff before it entered Lake George. The project came to a halt after crews from the museum's Cultural Resource Survey Program conducted an archeological survey with ground-penetrating radar and discovered prehistoric features and artifacts.

This stalled the construction project, and some 460 shovel test pits were dug initially, at twenty-five-foot intervals, to determine where the main sites might be. Later, another 45 test pits were dug in three principal areas (Million Dollar Beach A, B, and C). Much of the work subsequently focused on Million Dollar Beach A, where Early Archaic and Late Archaic components were found, and diagnostic projectile points included a chert Kanawaha point (Early Archaic) and a chert Normanskill point (Late Archaic). Site A had great integrity, with hearths and fire-cracked rocks, and excavations recovered over ten thousand flakes from tool manufacturing, along with numerous projectile points, bifaces, preforms, scrapers, hammerstones, drills, spokeshaves, and many cores.

The dig continued through the winter, with the archeologists working under tents, and the prehistoric components went to a depth of about one meter. The excavation was highly publicized (Lehman 2013a, 2013b, 2014), with local schoolchildren coming to visit. The biggest lesson to be learned from this dig was clearly that even areas that have been heavily used in modern times may still have extensive archeological remains lying just beneath the surface. The area surrounding the Million Dollar Beach has seen millions of visitors, and yet Native American campsites have survived, and here it was possible for them to be studied and protected.

THE LAKE GEORGE BATTLEFIELD PARK

The high ground at the southern end of Lake George now lies within the Lake George Battlefield Park, protected and made available to the public by the New York State Department of Environmental Conservation. Ever since SUNY Adirondack began excavations there in 2000, prehistoric artifacts have been found throughout the park, including projectile points, Middle Woodland pottery, and even a Meadowood cache blade (figs. 2.14 and 2.15).

However, it was not until the summer of 2016 that the most recent excavations in the park, on the west side of Fort George Road, uncovered a significant occupation from the late Middle Woodland or the early Late Woodland period. This was on a terrace that holds a commanding view of the southern end of Lake George, and we had already recovered hundreds of chert flakes running for hundreds of meters along Fort George Road. These were no doubt the by-product of the manufacture and re-sharpening of stone tools, but without diagnostic tools we had no means of assigning the flakes to a particular time period. Finally, it was in August that I found myself troweling in the yellowish-brown subsoil, about a foot beneath the surface. I was digging underneath a British officers' dump from the French and Indian War (to be discussed in

2.14. ▲
A Levanna point of chert shown *in situ* in the Lake George Battlefield Park in 2014. This point type is typical of the Late Woodland period.

2.15. ◄
A Meadowood cache blade of chert found in the Lake George Battlefield Park in 2014 and typical of the Early Woodland period.

chapter 3), and the military artifacts were pretty much exhausted. Now, however, I found myself brushing off a projectile point manufactured from chert that was about 1¼ inches long, the type that archeologists call Jack's Reef Corner-Notched. This point had once tipped the shaft of either a spear or an arrow, it was complete, and it was between one and two thousand years old. Even better, I found a second such point just two days later, only about a meter away (see fig. 2.16, bottom row). As it turned out, our British officers' dump lay directly on top of a prehistoric campsite that was much earlier, dating to a time when Native Americans entered the Adirondacks to hunt and fish.

2.16.
Top row: Middle Woodland pottery. *Bottom row:* Jack's Reef Corner-Notched points. All were found in the Lake George Battlefield Park on the west side of Fort George Road.

2.17.
A Snook Kill projectile point found in the Lake George Battlefield Park in 2016.

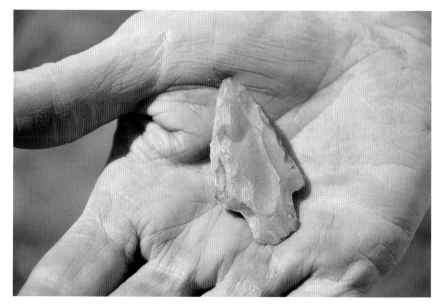

We excavated only a modest sample of this Middle Woodland site and did not locate any hearths or postholes, but clearly such sites may be found on the high terraces overlooking Lake George and not just on the shores of the lake. There also was ample prehistoric pottery (fig. 2.16, top row), as well as a stemmed projectile point (fig. 2.17), scrapers, and drills, but it is still too early to say whether there was an actual village site here.

Some Directions for Future Research

Archeological research is increasing in the Adirondacks, and an exciting new exhibition honoring Native Americans at Lake George and the larger Adirondack region has recently opened in the Native American room of the Lake George Historical Association (Adamson 2017). Native Americans are very much a part of this region today, and their history and contributions need to be presented to museum visitors as well as taught in local schools.

Part of the challenge, of course, is distinguishing among the contributions of Mohawks, Mohicans, and Abenakis. Each culture has played a very strong role in this region, and more should be done to identify the characteristics and significance of each.

Looking at the larger picture of human habitation in the Adirondacks reveals a long history in which native peoples proudly maintained their own cultures and identity while adapting to European influences after the 1600s. Fortunately, archeology conducted at early campsites and oral interviews among living peoples have both been extremely effective ways for all of us to grow in our knowledge and appreciation of native cultures, and with greater knowledge comes increased respect and admiration for the first Americans who occupied the Adirondack Mountains.

3.1.
Military reenactors
encamped at the
southern end of
Lake George in 2007.

FORTS AND BATTLEFIELDS

THREE

The Adirondack Mountains are known for their extensive forests, mines, and hiking trails, but generally not so much for dramatic military action. Nevertheless, along the eastern side of these mountains lie the remains of a great many eighteenth- and early nineteenth-century forts, battlefields, and military encampments that literally determined the future of our country. From Plattsburgh in the north to Lake George in the south, the north-south waterways that flank the Adirondacks provided a "great warpath" for invading armies (Starbuck 1999, 2011; Bellico 1992, 1995, 2010; Coffin, Curtis, and Curtis 2005; Calver and Bolton 1950). On the New York side of Lake Champlain and Lake George, military fortifications and remains may be found at Fort Saint-Frédéric, the adjacent British fort at Crown Point, Fort Ticonderoga, Fort William Henry, Fort Gage, throughout the Lake George Battlefield Park, and at smaller, more ephemeral blockhouses, outposts, and campsites. Just as important, the waterways contain numerous shipwrecks from the armies that relied upon water for the passage of their bateaux, whaleboats, and warships throughout the colonial wars (Zarzynski and Benway 2011).

From these easterly sites, military trails and roads were cut into the Adirondacks, providing some of the earliest European pathways into the mountains. While Ranger companies no doubt passed through this region (Todish 2002; Zaboly 2004), no archeologist has found even minor traces of Ranger activities in the interior of the Adirondacks. This may change one day, but the earliest military expeditions would have traveled light and would not have left substantial evidence behind that an enemy might track.

The region's military history continues to be relevant down to the present day as hundreds, and even thousands, of reenactors annually commemorate historic events at Fort Ticonderoga, Crown Point, and sites surrounding the southern end of Lake George (fig. 3.1). Many of these sites have been explored by archeologists, providing an exciting, hands-on experience for archeology students and volunteers every summer.

The sheer thrill of discovery can be the greatest experience of a lifetime, and I am reminded of one of my archeology students, Heather Thompson, running up to me with a fresh find in her hand in the summer of 2016 (fig. 3.2). She had just discovered a coin within a British officers' dump in the Lake George Battlefield Park, and she was beaming proudly as she showed it to me. Her

3.2.
The discovery of a 1766 British halfpenny in the Lake George Battlefield Park in 2016.

excitement, though, was not merely at finding a rare artifact. Rather, we had needed a means of dating the assemblage of stains and officer-quality artifacts found buried in a field overlooking Lake George, and the discovery of a 1766 British halfpenny was at least suggestive of a rare regimental camp created in the 1760s, in between the two major colonial wars of the eighteenth century. As I praised her rare find, we both were hoping to prove that our dump had been created during the shaky peacetime that preceded the American Revolution and the new battles and encampments that followed in the 1770s. This of course is exactly the sort of distinctive find that distinguishes modern archeology and demonstrates how the physical remains of the past have the ability to add very new stories to traditional history.

Archeology at the many military sites in the Adirondack region has been recounted quite extensively in other books, including *The Great Warpath*, *The Legacy of Fort William Henry*, and in other recent sources (Starbuck 1999, 2002b, 2010, 2014). For that reason, only broad outlines of those discoveries will be summarized here. However, many dramatic new finds have been made in the Lake George Battlefield Park over the past several years, and that work will receive much more intensive treatment in this volume.

3.3.
An exhibit devoted to the *Land Tortoise,* on display in the Underwater Archaeology Room at Fort William Henry. The scale model of the radeau (inside the display case) was constructed by John Farrell.

Underwater Discoveries

For many years, the group known as Bateaux Below worked to locate the remains of vessels on the bottom of Lake George, notably "the Sunken Fleet of 1758," now managed by New York State as a "Submerged Heritage Preserve." Unquestionably the greatest find made by Bateaux Below was the very intact hull of America's oldest extant wooden warship, the seven-sided, flat-bottomed radeau known as the *Land Tortoise,* which sank in 1758 (Zarzynski and Benway 2011; Starbuck 1999, chap. 8) (fig. 3.3). Just as important, the Lake Champlain Maritime Museum has located numerous shipwrecks in Lake Champlain, both from the French and Indian War and the American Revolution (Crisman 1986; Crisman and Cohn 1994). The cold water of both lakes has resulted in the excellent preservation of bateaux and other vessels, and these are exciting sights for sport divers. However, in nearly all cases, these watercraft need to remain *in situ* (preserved underwater where they have been found), given the extremely high costs of conservation for timbers and artifacts.

Crown Point

Some of the first military sites' archeology (or "conflict archeology") in this region occurred at Fort Saint-Frédéric, work that was briefly under the direction of Roland Robbins (Kravic 1971; Starbuck 1999, chap. 7). Fort Saint-Frédéric

3.4.
Barracks inside
the British fort at
Crown Point,
June 2017.

had been constructed by the French at the southern end of Lake Champlain to protect the movement of French settlers and traders into the Champlain Valley, and it was occupied between 1731 and 1759. Immediately after the departure of the French, the British under the leadership of General Jeffrey Amherst began construction of His Majesty's Fort at Crown Point (the British fort at Crown Point), adjacent to the ruins of Fort Saint-Frédéric (fig. 3.4).

This enormously important complex of archeological sites — including amazingly intact barracks buildings and earthworks — has seen many, many years of archeology. While others began excavations here early in the twentieth century, it was Paul Huey, Lois Feister (Huey), and Charles Fisher who truly made these sites their own, and they have published extensively on the remains. Paul Huey actually began digging here in 1956, at the age of fourteen, and continued digging many times over the years as senior archaeologist with New York State's Bureau of Historic Sites (Kourofsky 2009). For her part, Feister has used archeology to demonstrate status differences within the barracks buildings, while Fisher conducted notable work at hut sites nearby (Feister 1984a, 1984b, Fisher 1995). Fort Saint-Frédéric and the British fort at Crown Point both look out upon the new Lake Champlain Bridge, completed in 2011, and the expansive ruins of both forts are truly majestic set against the backdrop of Lake Champlain.

Fort Ticonderoga

Of the many very special military sites in New York State dating to both the French and Indian War and the American Revolution, one of the most distinguished is Fort Ticonderoga, which overlooks both Lake Champlain and the outlet of Lake George. From 1755, when it was first constructed as Fort Carillon, down to the present day, Ticonderoga has seen many battles, occupations by a variety of armies, extensive encampments, and an early opening (1909) to the public as one of our country's greatest military attractions. While artifacts were collected during the reconstruction of Fort Ticonderoga early in the twentieth century, it was not until 1957 that J. Duncan Campbell excavated the French village nearby in what might be considered the first true archeology at that site (Campbell 1958). Later, nautical archeologists conducted excavations here in Fort Ticonderoga's King's Shipyard (Krueger et al. 1985).

The most recent archeological work at Fort Ticonderoga was a contract project conducted by Hartgen Archeological Associates (directed by Elise Manning-Sterling and Bruce Sterling), who dug in 2001 and 2005 along the eastern side of the fort in advance of the construction of the Deborah Clark Mars Education Center (fig. 3.5). The extensive grounds that surround Fort Ticonderoga contain the remains of many French and British encampments, as well as Native American sites, and there is enormous potential here for future archeological research.

3.5.
The Deborah Clark Mars Education Center at Fort Ticonderoga.

3.6.
The modern parade
ground of Fort
William Henry.

Fort William Henry

Perhaps credit for the very first military site archeology within the Adirondack
Park belongs to Fort William Henry (1755–1757) on Lake George, where Stanley Gifford directed excavations from 1953 to 1954 (Gifford 1955). This fort was
the basis for James Fenimore Cooper's novel *The Last of the Mohicans* ([1826]
1980), and Gifford's excavation was a necessary prelude to reconstruction of
the fort, which opened to the public in 1955 (fig. 3.6). His team recovered large
numbers of artifacts from the northwest bastion of the fort (which was excavated completely), and Gifford also exposed numerous skeletons of soldiers
both inside and outside the remains of the fort (see chapter 7). These human
remains were studied by forensic anthropologists and removed from public
display between 1993 and 1995 (Liston and Baker 1995; Baker and Rieth 2000).
A new series of excavations then commenced at Fort William Henry in 1997,
and seven seasons of excavations have occurred since then (1997–2000 and
2011–2013), led by David Starbuck and working with field teams from SUNY
Adirondack (Starbuck 1990, 1993, 1998, 1999, 2002b, 2008, 2014).

Fort William Henry has seen intensive excavations in the cellars of barracks
buildings located in the parade ground, and also much work in the dumps on
the eastern side of the fort. Even the 1756 well inside the fort was excavated
in 1997 (Starbuck 2001). Because the French burned and leveled this log fort
in 1757, Fort William Henry would never have become the major tourist attraction it is today if it were not for extensive archeological documentation.

A snapshot showing the excavation of Fort Gage in 1975. Courtesy of Carolyn Weatherwax.

The combination of contemporary military records, foundations exposed by archeologists, and rich artifact deposits has permitted the rebuilding and interpretation of the British fort that suffered the most during the French and Indian War.

Fort Gage

Just southwest of the modern village of Lake George, the impending construction of a Ramada Inn close to the Adirondack Northway (Interstate 87) led to the salvage excavation that was conducted in May and June of 1975 at Fort Gage, the first fort to be built after the destruction of Fort William Henry (fig. 3.7). In work directed by Paul Huey and Lois Feister, with members of the Auringer-Seelye Chapter of the New York State Archaeological Association, the remains of this 1758 fort needed to be rescued in a matter of days. In spite of limited time and no budget whatever, the quality of the excavations and record-keeping easily exceeded everything that had come before in the Lake George area (Feister and Huey 1985). Sadly, very little remains of this fort today.

Birch Avenue in Lake George

An important cultural resources investigation was conducted very close to Fort Gage by the "Birch Avenue Archeology Project," undertaken between 1993 and 1997. Also located southwest of the village of Lake George, this excavation by Collamer and Associates, directed in the field by Sarah Majot, exposed brief

3.8.
Burned stains from military
camps on Birch Avenue.
Courtesy of Sarah Majot and
ARCH TECH.

French and Indian War encampment sites across a broad area that was about
to be disturbed by the construction of a substation for the Niagara Mohawk
Power Corporation (fig. 3.8). Rich scatters of artifacts and cultural features
were found throughout wooded areas where artifact collectors had been metal-
detecting for years. This proved to be yet another vitally important rescue
effort, and the final report on this work was recipient of a 1998 New York State
Historic Preservation Award.

Until quite recently, sites created by American forces during the War of
1812 did not receive as much attention locally by historical archeologists as did
the earlier forts and battlefields of the eighteenth century. Fortunately that is
now changing, especially with work at Cantonment Saranac in Plattsburgh
between 2011 and 2013. At this particular site, Tim Abel and students from
Clinton Community College discovered remains from Colonel Zebulon Pike's
winter cantonment of 1812–13 (Abel 2015a) and "unearthed a nearly complete
soldier's cabin, possibly occupied by a field officer of the 15th Regiment of In-
fantry" (Abel 2016, 58). Abel also conducted archeology between 2004 and
2012 with students and volunteers at Storrs Harbor, a War of 1812 naval shipyard located just west of the Adirondack Park (Abel 2015b).

Previously, most of the archeological research on the War of 1812 had been conducted elsewhere in the eastern United States, and fortunately some of that work has now appeared in recent syntheses (Lucas and Schablitsky 2016; *Northeast Historical Archaeology*, 2015). However, it is now clear that from Plattsburgh and the Adirondacks north to the Canadian border, there is enormous potential for some of the best War of 1812 archeology in the country. Abel and his colleagues have exciting work ahead of them.

New Research in the Lake George Battlefield Park

The ruins of several of the most intact eighteenth-century military encampments in North America lie atop a bluff overlooking the southern end of Lake George, high above the Million Dollar Beach. Now overgrown with trees, yet nicely interpreted with trails, signboards, and monuments, the Lake George Battlefield Park has been the setting for some of the most recent archeological research in the region, and it is easily one of the last relatively untouched military sites along the historic corridor that runs from New York City to Canada. Totally unspoiled by commercial development, yet within easy walking distance of the village of Lake George, Battlefield Park is outstanding among historical attractions in its quiet ambiance and scenic beauty. It is exciting to walk under the pine trees and imagine the eighteenth-century battle, the fort, and the encampments that once dominated this hilltop. We archeologists and historians are not alone in our enthusiasm for the park, and nearby residents regularly walk their dogs here, even as thousands of visitors come to hike, jog, bicycle, picnic, and enjoy the historic ruins. The residents of Lake George quietly appreciate, and seek to protect, what is unquestionably some of the most hallowed ground in the Adirondacks.

Today the Lake George Battlefield Park is carefully managed by the New York State Department of Environmental Conservation (DEC), which has been custodian of this complex of sites since 1898. A tour road enters the park on the southwest from Fort George Road and winds past military ruins and picnic tables until it reaches the northern promontory, where it is possible to look down through the trees toward the Million Dollar Beach and the waters of Lake George. The park contains traces of the battle of Lake George, where on September 8, 1755, British forces under General William Johnson fought a French army led by Baron Dieskau, the first major battle fought between the British and French in what is now northern New York State. The British carried the day, prompting James Fenimore Cooper's fictional hero, Hawkeye, to comment in *The Last of the Mohicans*: "Hundreds of Frenchmen saw the sun that day for the last time; and even their leader, Dieskau himself, fell into our hands, so cut and torn with the lead that he has gone back to his own country, unfit for further acts in war" (Cooper [1826] 1980, chap. 14).

The battle of Lake George was followed by the hasty construction of Fort William Henry, Fort Edward, and Fort Carillon (Ticonderoga), as the French and British jockeyed for advantage and control of the vital waterways. Later, as Fort William Henry was attacked and fell to the French in August 1757, these grounds held an entrenched camp of about eighteen hundred British soldiers and militia who had rushed to the defense of the fort, but who themselves fell victim to the onslaught by the French forces led by the Marquis de Montcalm. After the surrender of Fort William Henry on August 9, the entrenched camp was repeatedly assaulted by Indians on August 10, and the defenseless, surrendered garrison then fell prey to Montcalm's Indian allies as it marched down the military road toward Fort Edward with a minimal French escort.

The park also has many foundations left behind by the sizable British army that camped here in 1758 under the command of General James Abercrombie, who subsequently failed that summer to take Fort Carillon from the French. The most visible remains of all are those of Fort George and its many outbuildings, constructed in 1759 by the army of General Jeffrey Amherst just before it occupied Fort Carillon, which had been blown up by the retreating French. It was in July of that year that Amherst eyed this hilltop and delegated the construction of Fort George to Colonel James Montresor of the Royal Engineers (Kochan 1993). Fort George thus became the principal base from which to attack the French in the north, and while only the southwest bastion of this stone fort was ever completed, the British did construct a smaller wooden stockade of three bastions, along with barracks, hospitals, storehouses, and other buildings.

Engineers' maps from the late 1750s reveal dozens of structures covering this hilltop (fig. 3.9), and the huge British base was still occupied by a small garrison in 1775 when American patriots under Captain Bernard Romans captured the fort. In the months that followed, General Philip Schuyler established regulations for American soldiers here, and extensive smallpox hospitals were constructed nearby, probably the largest concentration of smallpox hospitals and patients in North America. Between two and three thousand soldiers were also sent here after the disastrous American invasion of Canada at the end of 1775.

Fort George changed hands yet again in July of 1777 when General John Burgoyne approached, en route to his battle with Patriot forces in Old Saratoga (now Schuylerville, New York). American forces burned Fort George in anticipation of his arrival and retreated to Fort Edward. Fort George then became one of the supply points that linked Burgoyne with Canada in the months that followed.

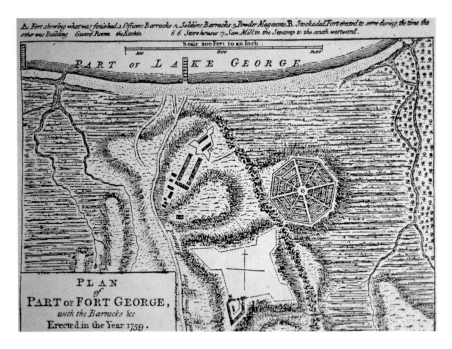

A: Fort shewing what was finished 1 Officers Barracks 2 Soldiers Barracks 3 Powder Magazine B: Stockaded Fort erected to serve during the time the other was Building. Guard Room. the Kitchin. 66 Storehouses 7 Saw Mill in the Swamp to the south westward.

Scale 200 Feet to an Inch

PART OF LAKE GEORGE.

PLAN
of
PART of FORT GEORGE,
with the Barracks &c
Erected in the Year 1759.

The final action at this site occurred in October 1780 when an American garrison consisting of Captain Thomas Sill and a small group of Vermonters came under attack by a British raiding party led by Major Christopher Carleton. The Vermonters were forced to surrender, the fort was burned, and an American militiaman, George Fowler, has provided us with a chilling account of the aftermath: "We marched on up to Fort George which had been burned by the enemy who had just gone down the lake. The beams and other timbers of the fort were still smoking and burning when we arrived. The bodies of twelve men were found lying where they fell—scalped and shockingly mangled, bloated and black with partial mortification. It was a most horrid sight."

This ended the use of Fort George as a military base, but nineteenth-century travelers often stayed in the surviving buildings. Even General George Washington visited in 1783, followed by James Madison and Thomas Jefferson in 1791.

Fort George and the rest of the Lake George Battlefield Park has never been built upon since then, but twenty-five years of continuous construction and conflict had left foundations scattered across the surface of the park. These are the only fortifications on Lake George to span both major wars of the eighteenth century. In recognition of the site's unique significance, the thirteen-foot-high Lake George Battle Monument was erected at the northern end of the park in 1903 by the Society of Colonial Wars, with statues honoring

William Johnson and his English ally King Hendrick of the Mohawks, the latter of whom died at the battle of Lake George (fig. 3.10). A bronze statue of a Native American, functioning as a fountain (dedicated in 1921), stands a short distance to the south. The southwest bastion of Fort George twice saw stabilization work in the twentieth century, and the ruins of the fort are easily the most prominent military feature in the park (fig. 3.11). However, depressions and foundation stones from dozens of military buildings cover the surface of the park, revealing where British and American military encampments lay in the 1750s and 1770s (fig. 3.12).

The interpretation of Fort George and the Battlefield Park has really only just begun. While sites on private land have often seen many years of digging by archeologists and collectors, few have received protection by the State of New York, and only Fort George was totally off-limits to archeology until very recently. The Battlefield Park offers exciting research opportunities because it holds the remains of a battle, the ruins of barracks and huts that had been occupied by at least ten thousand soldiers and officers, and even a fort that, if completed, would have become the largest British fort in North America.

I received a permit from the New York State Department of Environmental Conservation in 1994 that permitted SUNY Adirondack to begin mapping the surface of the Battlefield Park. A few years later, the members of Bateaux Below conducted historical research that resulted in the creation of excellent interpretive signboards along the tour road that runs through the park. Later, I received permits in 2000 and 2001 from the DEC and the New York State Museum to conduct the first professional archeology in the park (Starbuck 2002a). Those early efforts were followed up more recently by summer field schools in 2014, 2015, and 2016, with SUNY Adirondack responsible for uncovering remains from an amazing variety of military sites that appear to be more intact than many others in our region.

In the summer of 2000 we dug into the clearly visible foundations of two of the barracks buildings that General Amherst had constructed there in 1759, as well as several lesser sites. In the process, we discovered well-preserved walls and tremendous numbers of artifacts from both the French and Indian War and the American Revolution. These first foundations to be studied were solidly constructed of mortared limestone, and the overlying soil was often two feet deep or more. These foundations were located inside what was formerly a wood stockade of three bastions at the northern edge of the bluff that overlooks Lake George. From engineers' maps prepared in the 1750s, we knew that this fortification had contained two small barracks buildings and was the front line of defense while the main fort, Fort George, was being constructed about six hundred feet to the south. Because natural bedrock juts through the

3.10. ◀
The Lake George Battle Monument, portraying
General William Johnson and King Hendrick,
leader of the Mohawks.

3.11. ▼
The sole surviving corner bastion of Fort George.
Its appearance reflects the restoration work done
there in the twentieth century.

3.12. ◀
Stones from build-
ing foundations on
the surface of Lake
George Battlefield
Park. Lake George is
just out of view in
the rear.

3.13. ▲
Excavating a barracks foundation in the summer of 2000. This is all that remains from an officers' barracks that originally stood within a wood stockade in 1759.

3.14. ▶
An engraved hinge from a chest, inscribed "Achmuty of the . . ." This was discovered on the edge of the officers' barracks (fig. 3.13) excavated in 2000.

surface of the Battlefield Park in many places, we were surprised and delighted to discover sites so deeply buried and undisturbed.

The more northerly of these barracks foundations measured 17 by 67 feet, and inside we discovered great quantities of fallen wall plaster, suggesting that it may have been an officers' barracks (fig. 3.13). The second foundation, less finished in appearance, may have been for a structure that housed enlisted men. We also found thousands of pottery sherds and animal bones from the soldiers' meals (including fish bones likely from Lake George); many buttons (including numbered regimental buttons), a four-pound cannonball, musket parts, hinges, wine bottles, medicine bottles, a spade, a single strip of gold braid from a uniform, and even the hinge from a chest that bore the inscribed name of an officer, "Achmuty" (fig. 3.14). This probably belonged to Lieutenant Thomas Achmuty of the Twenty-Seventh (Inniskilling) Regiment (George Bray, personal communication, Sept. 22, 2014).

In the next season, 2001, we examined a far larger number of huts and barracks and even placed several test pits inside the one surviving bastion of Fort George. Once again we relied very heavily on the British engineers' maps from the late 1750s, and these helped lead us to the foundations of at least eight or ten additional buildings. We excavated small numbers of pits in each of these, as well as in dumps and earthworks, and in doing so we discovered that nearly all had been occupied during both the French and Indian War and the American Revolution. Each feature had been drawn on the 1750s maps, but each also contained numbered regimental buttons and sherds of creamware that would not have been in use until the Revolution. This suggested that the original 1750s buildings were still in good enough condition twenty years later that they could be repaired and used by the next occupying army.

The distinctive artifacts that we found in 2001 included a well-preserved brass pocket sundial and compass with the Roman numerals "XXIX" scratched onto the case, probably indicating that someone from the British Twenty-Ninth Regiment of Foot had lost this valuable compass while based here during the American Revolution (fig. 3.15). We also found the ruptured barrel from a British "Brown Bess" musket, a lead weight, buttons of the Twenty-Sixth Regiment, stems from wineglasses, a very intact door lock mechanism, a complete bayonet, and a stock clasp of brass so finely made that it could only have come from an officer's uniform. With discoveries such as these comes the obligation to provide for their conservation so that artifacts that have lain in the ground for hundreds of years do not deteriorate the moment they are introduced to a new storage environment. Fortunately many of these finds have recently been conserved through the auspices of the New York State Museum (fig. 3.16).

There is a danger in over-digging such sensitive, important sites, and we halted our excavations after the 2001 season and did not return to the Lake George Battlefield Park until 2014. This did not happen until after many discussions with officials from the New York State Museum and the Department of Environmental Conservation, at which times we reviewed priorities, field and laboratory methods, and research questions. We then resumed our research for another three field seasons (2014–2016), once again with field schools sponsored by SUNY Adirondack and with permits issued by the New York State Museum.

Throughout the summer of 2014, we principally tested barracks and hut sites that had been occupied by British forces in 1759. This was done partially to better differentiate between French and Indian War occupations and those of the American Revolution, and a primary objective was to help visitors to

3.15.
A brass pocket sundial and compass discovered in a hut site in 2001, now housed in the collections of the New York State Museum.

3.16.
An assortment of conserved artifacts from the Lake George Battlefield Park, now in the New York State Museum.

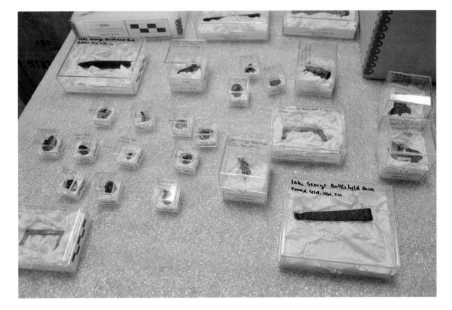

better understand the exact locations of the park's many occupations and battles over a twenty-five-year period. We found ourselves excavating Revolutionary War dumps atop French and Indian War sites, and two dumps were located that contained remains from the British Sixtieth Regiment of Foot, which was in residence between the two wars (ca. 1768–1772) (fig. 3.17).

In 2015 we finally were ready to begin a more thorough exploration of the remains of Fort George. The construction of this British fort by Colonel

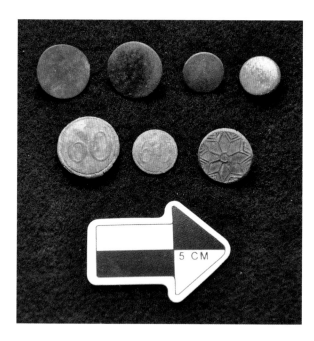

3.17.
Buttons found in two dumps in 2014. Two buttons of the British Sixtieth Regiment of Foot appear in the bottom row, left and center.

Montresor began in the summer of 1759 on the orders of General Amherst, who commanded an eleven-thousand-man army. If completed, it would have become the largest British fort in North America. However, Amherst's army successfully took Fort Carillon (Ticonderoga) that summer, and only one enormous corner bastion was actually completed. This bastion contained a solitary barracks building, and other rooms were added and occupied in later years as British and colonial armies came and went (fig. 3.18). As already mentioned, the final destruction of Fort George came in 1780 at the hands of Christopher Carleton's raiding party from Canada.

The ruins of Fort George often received visitors, until finally a substantial stabilization effort occurred in the 1920s. Now managed within the Lake George Battlefield Park by the State of New York, the scenic ruins of Fort George are an annual attraction for the hundreds of thousands of summer visitors to Lake George. Still, until recently there was no awareness of what might have survived from the barracks or later construction, even though this had become known as the only British fort on Lake George to have spanned both major eighteenth-century wars.

Our pits placed inside the fort's bastion in 2001 had revealed some evidence for stone walls, but we needed to see much more if we were to understand the overall interior layout. Digs at other, contemporary British sites on Lake George and in nearby Fort Edward had revealed only the charred remains of log walls from the short-term forts that dotted the British frontier in the 1750s.

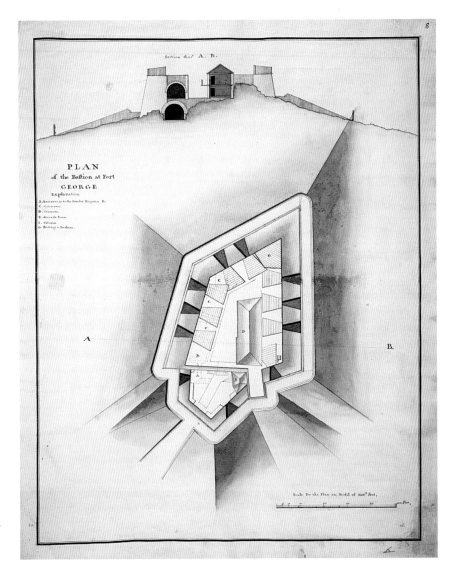

3.18.
"Plan of the Bastion at Fort George." This shows the sole bastion of Fort George, revealing the central barracks building and a series of interior rooms around the perimeter. Norman B. Leventhal Map Center, Boston. Original is in the British Library.

This did not prepare us for the substantial, well-mortared stone walls that we exposed in 2015 inside the bastion of Fort George, where British and colonial soldiers had sheltered themselves for at least twenty-two years (fig. 3.19). What we found were belowground cellar rooms — probably for the storage of supplies and munitions — and these were surrounded by walls nearly five feet thick and at least six feet high. While modern tourist artifacts were abundant in the shallower soil layers, much collapsed building debris (quarried stones and mortar) lay underneath. Finally, at the very base of the stone walls, scattered atop the natural bedrock, we discovered soldiers' artifacts that included tin-glazed earthenware pottery sherds, buttons, butchered bones, musket

3.19.
Belowground stone walls within the sole surviving bastion of Fort George being excavated in 2015.

balls, and gun flints. The solitary lives of British and American soldiers on the northern frontier of colonial America were now becoming a little bit clearer, and we found ourselves looking upon one of the few settings in northern New York where the British army built relatively permanent architecture. We were fortunate at the end of the season when "shock inmates" from the state corrections facility at Moriah were brought in to fill our pits with sandbags.

During the 2016 field season, we returned to the surviving bastion of Fort George, but this time we focused on the remains of the interior barracks building that had been constructed by Amherst's army in 1759 (and which was subsequently occupied through 1780). We uncovered foundation walls at the northernmost end of the barracks (fig. 3.20), digging down to bedrock and removing rubble fill that consisted of bricks, mortar, and stones. Atop where the floor must originally have been we discovered the complete mandible (jaw) from a moose, the first archeological evidence for moose that we have ever found in the region (fig. 3.21). At the conclusion of the 2016 excavation, our own team of archeologists did the filling of hundreds of sandbags and placed them alongside the walls to ensure maximum stability of the structural remains, essential if the barracks foundation is to be seen by future generations.

The ruins of Fort George have always been the most visible — and the most-visited — feature within the Battlefield Park, but nothing prepared us for a final surprise during the 2016 field season. On the western side of Fort George Road (which runs from Canada Street/Route 9 northeast to Beach Road in Lake George), archeological testing had never been conducted in the large,

3.20.
Documenting the walls at the northern end of the barracks building inside Fort George.

3.21.
Exposing a moose jaw (just to the left of the archeologist) inside the barracks in Fort George.

open fields that run down to the Million Dollar Beach and the waters of Lake George. We knew that parking lots had formerly been located there, that utility lines ran through the fields, and that numerous encampments of reenactors had set up there in recent years. Still, we were curious as to whether there might still be some traces of encampments from the eighteenth century, and so we proceeded to excavate a row of pits across one of the fields.

While testing a totally new area may have felt like a long shot, it was incredibly exciting to then discover the dark staining from an extensive dump that was virtually intact, right on the side of the highway (fig. 3.22). It contained substantial quantities of pottery and porcelain (fig. 3.23); a brass watch winder (fig. 3.24); literally thousands of butchered bone fragments (cow, pig, sheep, and fish); large oyster shells that must have been transported at least two hundred miles from the seacoast up the Hudson River and then by land to Lake George (fig. 3.25); many fragments of wine bottles and wineglasses; numerous hand-wrought nails; and even part of a three-legged pipkin (an earthenware cooking pot). Just as surprising was the discovery of a horse tooth (fig. 3.26), which, just like the moose mandible, was the first we have found in any of our excavations at eighteenth-century military sites in New York State. (Given the abundance of bones here from more traditional food sources, it would appear this tooth had been a souvenir, perhaps carried by an officer as a reminder of his favorite horse.)

The high quality of the ceramic vessels suggests that this dump contained the trash from officers' dwellings, and the presence of a 1766 British halfpenny (fig. 3.27) further suggests that this may have been a dump from one of the regiments that occupied the park at a time between the major wars. This was only about two hundred feet from the dump excavated in 2014 that contained the British Sixtieth Regiment of Foot buttons, and that regimental encampment may well have been the source for this high-quality trash. It was definitely a kitchen-related deposit, with few musket balls or gun flints. In its own curious

3.22.
Archeological testing in 2016 on the western side of Fort George Road.

3.23. ▶
Several of the molded sherds of white salt-glazed stoneware found in the dump west of Fort George Road. While a few decorative plate sherds have been discovered in other contexts, the presence here of fragments from a sugar bowl was quite unusual.

3.24. ▶▶
A Georgian-period brass watch winder found in the dump in 2016. It measures just over one inch high and weighs just 3.8 grams.

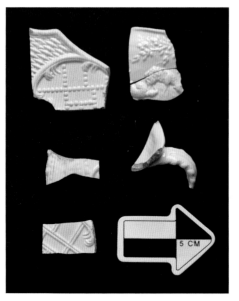

3.25. ▲
A few of the oyster shells found in the dump west of Fort George Road.

3.26. ▶
The horse's molar found in the dump west of Fort George Road. Contrary to popular opinion, horse bones are rarely found on historical sites.

3.27.
A 1766 British halfpenny found in the dump west of Fort George Road. This well-preserved copper coin is a rare survival that dates to the decade in between the two major eighteenth-century wars.

way, it is really quite charming to imagine British officers casually eating and dining this well just ten years after the disaster that occurred at Fort William Henry less than a mile away.

The Battlefield Park is slowly coming into its own as a truly major military attraction on Lake George, and it has survived so well because the Department of Environmental Conservation, local residents, and most recently the Fort George Alliance (a Friends group) have worked extremely hard to protect its integrity and ensure that modern development does not disturb these exciting ruins. All these constituencies are eager for the park to receive visitors, and the ruins and artifacts must be preserved so that those who come after us will have the same opportunity to understand what an eighteenth-century military encampment looked like. Everything here is original — nothing is a twenty-first-century re-creation of the past — and all the constituent groups would like to keep it that way.

4.1.
Blast furnace stack of the "New Furnace" at the site
of the Upper Works of the Adirondack Iron and Steel
Company in Tahawus (2016); this rose some forty-five
feet when completed in 1854, and it operated for only
two years. Made of blocks of stone reinforced with iron
tie rods, it is also referred to as the McIntyre Furnace.

INDUSTRIAL RUINS IN THE ADIRONDACKS

The forests of the Adirondacks contain the remains of sawmills, furnaces, ore pits, dams, bridges, brickworks, train tracks, charcoal mounds, tanneries, kilns, and quarries, and no doubt many other types of industrial ruins as well. This may seem ironic, given the region's reputation for wilderness, old-growth forest, and environmental conservation at the highest levels, but the Adirondacks are exceptionally rich in both natural and mineral resources, and early visitors came here in search of work. Thanks to the isolation of many of these sites, they were never raided for scrap during the world wars, and much of the old metal from past industries remains in place, along with the stone foundations (Charles Vandrei, personal communication, Aug. 11, 2016). To a visitor traveling through the mountains, the overall effect is quite striking, as the largest, most pristine forest in the eastern United States shelters hundreds of crumbling, decaying, industrial structures. Outdoor recreation may explain the two hundred thousand seasonal residents in the Adirondacks today, but it was industry and timber harvesting that originally defined the region.

Extractive industries have been especially prominent in the Adirondacks, and no community has a greater legacy than Tahawus (Hochschild 1962c; Gereau 2014), a source of extensive deposits of titanium dioxide and home of the Adirondack Iron and Steel Company, which operated between 1826 and 1857. The Historic American Engineering Record (HAER) conducted an excellent survey at the industrial ruins in Tahawus in 1978, and their photographs and drawings have been housed ever since at both the U.S. Library of Congress and the Adirondack Experience on Blue Mountain Lake. Located in the High Peaks district, Adirondack Iron and Steel utilized titaniferous iron ore, with charcoal as the fuel, and the blast furnaces here were the centerpiece of a complex in Tahawus that included "a combined church and school, some 25 houses, a massive wooden boarding house, an ice house, carpenter shop, blacksmith shop, saw mill, grist mill, and power house" (Seely 1981, 29). The stack of the surviving "New Furnace," constructed between 1849 and 1854, is wonderfully well preserved (fig. 4.1), a sharp contrast from the collapsed 1844 furnace a short distance away in the abandoned community of Adirondac (fig. 4.7). A great many early furnaces are now little more than piles of stones, and the New Furnace is one of the most intact nineteenth-century iron ore furnaces in the United States.

The study by HAER involved intensive historical research and physical documentation of the surviving remains of this remote ironworks, including a superb set of measured drawings of the New Furnace, as well as reconstruction drawings of the blowing engine and hearth. In conducting this study, HAER helped to demonstrate how the charcoal iron industry — using old technological processes — still competed quite successfully with the new mineral fuels (chiefly coal) that were revolutionizing the industry. Fieldwork at the site has been continued by others down to the present day, notably by the Cultural Resource Survey Program at the New York State Museum (Staley 2012, 2016).

A modern visit to the remains at Tahawus, about sixteen miles from the town of Newcomb in the heart of the Adirondacks, is little short of breathtaking, given the number of industrial survivals at that site (figs. 4.2 to 4.7). No other industrial ruin in the Adirondacks is presented to the public in such a clear and informative way, with interpretive panels that not only identify the function of a structure, but also clearly present the industrial processes involved. The Adirondack Iron and Steel site offers the sort of rich storytelling that is enjoyed by industrial archeologists, among others who want to understand how the equipment was actually operated. Credit for this wonderful presentation goes to the Open Space Institute and the New York State Department of Environmental Conservation. They have taken a formidable set of ruins and created an impressive, eloquent monument to our industrial past.

The Iron Industry Elsewhere in the Adirondacks

After the very successful HAER recording project in Tahawus, studies were initiated by James Dawson of SUNY Plattsburgh and others at the many bloomery forges in the Adirondacks, where iron ore was "reduced directly to solid iron with charcoal fuel in a hearth that is small enough to be worked by one person" (Allen et al. 1990, 3). Thirty-two bloomery forges have been identified as operating in the Adirondacks in the nineteenth century, the largest of which was in Clintonville, where a bloomery forge built in 1810 grew into an operation employing nearly nine hundred workers. Gordon Pollard, now professor emeritus from SUNY Plattsburgh, spent four field seasons there between 1994 and 2001, documenting the ironworks with his students. Altogether, Clintonville had some sixteen bloomery forges inside the main forge building, and these date to a time when Clintonville had "the largest charcoal iron forge in the world" (Pollard and Klaus 2004). Pollard conducted extensive and highly successful excavations at the Lower Forge site in Clintonville, easily the most thorough archeology that has been conducted at any industrial site in the Adirondacks.

While it has not been the object of archeological study, special mention should be given to Benson Mines in the town of Clifton, on the western side of

4.2. ▲
A tuyere arch of the New Furnace in Tahawus.

4.3. ◄
A view of the lining of the New Furnace.

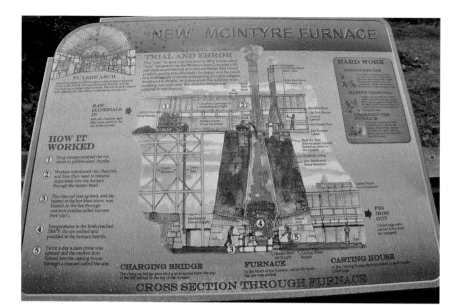

4.4.
An interpretive panel showing how the New Furnace operated.

4.5.
Some of the abandoned equipment resting near the New Furnace.

the Adirondacks, which in the 1950s was home to the largest open pit iron-ore mine in the world (Hall 2005; Carl 2009; Bramen 2017). The magnetite ore at Benson Mines was discovered in 1810 by engineers conducting a survey for a new highway, and beginning in 1889 the Carthage and Adirondack Railroad transported great quantities of ore from this mine, continuing up until World War I. The mine resumed operation in World War II and provided ore until 1977, when it finally closed. Today the mine is chiefly known for associated

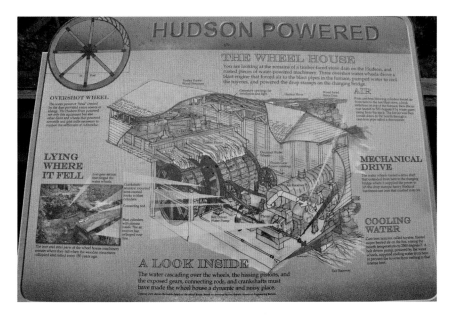

4.6.
An interpretive panel showing how water flowed through the wheelhouse next to the New Furnace.

4.7.
The 1844 furnace at Adirondac. The adjacent interpretive panel identifies this as "the last of several furnaces built within the village of Adirondac." Today it is literally a pile of stone rubble.

environmental degradation, contaminated soil, and abandoned buildings, and no cleanup appears likely in the near future. The fifty-four-acre industrial complex appears to have every likely type of pollution: "Concrete block buildings have collapsed floors and roofs. Steel I-beams are exposed, windows broken, interiors gutted and yawning holes are left in walls where machinery was removed. The landscape between buildings is littered with machine parts, asphalt, piles of ore, concrete fragments and scrap metal" (Carl 2009, 78). Will this someday be treated as an archeological site? Perhaps. After all, modern-day archeologists are often involved in cleanup efforts, and the Benson Mines — in spite of being arguably the most polluted site in the Adirondacks — will still need to be physically documented once a cleanup actually begins.

There are many other sites of abandoned ironworks throughout the Adirondacks that would benefit greatly from archeological surveys. One of these is in the village of Ironville, about thirteen miles west of Lake Champlain. Iron ore was found in the vicinity in 1826 (fig. 4.8), and Ironville became one of many communities in Essex County that formed because of the iron industry. A forge with two bloomery hearths was built here in 1828, drawing ore from several local mines; sawmills and gristmills were constructed; and later "a large ore separator was built to process ore for both the forge and the anthracite-fired blast furnaces that were put up by the Crown Point Iron Company on the shores of Lake Champlain" (Allen et al. 1990, 11).

The mines in the nearby village of Hammondville, the ore separator in Ironville (then called Irondale), and the blast furnaces on Lake Champlain were all connected by a thirteen-mile-long narrow-gauge railway built by the Crown Point Iron Company. The forges in Ironville steadily enlarged until 1879, at which time there were eight hearths, but by four years later they had closed down. These were all company towns that had rapidly grown in population, but when the depression of 1893 caused the Crown Point Iron Company to close, most of the workers left the region, leaving behind the ruins of forges, slag piles, headraces and tailraces, and open mine shafts.

Slightly farther to the north, beds of iron ore were discovered in Moriah (Port Henry), and more nineteenth-century company towns formed in Mineville and Witherbee, later becoming Republic Steel. The iron mines saw a resurgence in the mid-twentieth century as Mineville once again produced millions of tons of ore, but this was short-lived. There are no indications that the mining of iron will ever return to the Adirondacks.

The Ironville Historic District was listed on the National Register of Historic Places in 1974, and today Ironville features exhibits and publications on the history of the local iron industry (fig. 4.9). This includes an attractive walking trail with ten stops with signboards and several exposed industrial foundations, all administered by the Penfield Homestead Museum (fig. 4.10). The Penfield Foundation has done a wonderful job in preserving local industrial sites, and every village in the area celebrates its involvement in the early iron industry. A fascinating aura surrounds Hammondville in particular, which is locally referred to as an "Essex County ghost town" (Pope n.d.). While access is tightly restricted, the abandoned town has many deep mine shafts, and it is unquestionably the iron mining site that future archeologists will most want to document.

4.8.
Iron ore and slag from Ironville, from the collection of Eileen Klymn.

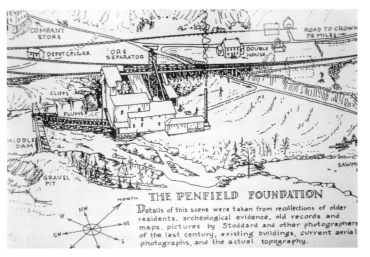

4.9.
A re-creation of part of the iron-works in Ironville. Prepared by the Penfield Foundation.

4.10.
A "stone lined pit [that] marks the location of the scale used to weigh ore cars coming from the mines at Hammondville, three miles to the west." This is Station 4 on the Historic Walking Trail created by the Penfield Homestead Museum.

The abandoned town of Graphite (see chapter 1) was easily the most exciting of the many communities that participated in the graphite industry (Ross 1976). The mineral graphite, best-known as a writing tool (the pencil) and machine lubricant, was discovered here in West Hague in 1887, and it achieved fame when used to make Dixon's "Ticonderoga pencils." The town of Graphite was home to the largest graphite mine in the world, but today the site is covered with forest, sprinkled with the ruins and cellar holes of numerous buildings, both domestic and industrial. After the town's abandonment in 1921, salvage efforts left only the belowground portions of buildings intact, but modern visitors are able to see mine tunnels, part of the crushing mill, and even ordinary house foundations (figs. 4.11 to 4.16). Railroad tracks are still visible inside the mine, and carts loaded with graphite would have traveled downhill from there to the mill. In recent years, research has also been conducted at other graphite mines in the Adirondack region, for example at the mines and mills of the Graphite Products Corporation in the towns of Wilton and Greenfield (Weatherwax 2008), but the ruins in the town of Graphite are especially impressive.

Other Types of Mining in the Adirondacks

While iron mining in the Adirondacks has always received the most attention from archeologists and others, the nineteenth century also saw mines in the region that produced galena (lead), pyrite, graphite, garnet, gypsum, and talc. However, by the early and mid-twentieth century, all types of mining were declining, and some — such as graphite mining — ceased altogether. There was successful mining of titanium dioxide in Tahawus by the National Lead Company up until 1989, and some mining of gypsum in the Adirondacks up until 1999, but extremely few mines operate in the region today.

One very prominent exception to this long-term pattern of decline is Barton Mines, which produces the largest garnets in the world and is a leading supplier of abrasives throughout the world (D. Johnson 1993). Barton Mines was established in 1878 by Henry Hudson Barton, and the original mine operated in North Creek for 104 years near the summit of Gore Mountain. In 1982, the operations were moved to neighboring Ruby Mountain, where the company still operates today. It may appear to some that we archeologists would rather see a company go out of business so that we can begin to study it, but that is certainly not the case here. All the other mines and associated buildings and dumps may one day collapse and become available for us to document, but we would much rather see an operation like Barton Mines continue to be wonderfully successful.

4.11.
"The open pit mine in Graphite." From *Dixon Plumbago Mine—1890*. Dixon's American Graphite Company Mine, Graphite, Hague Township, Warren County, New York.

4.12.
One of the entrances to the graphite mine at Graphite in 2017, blocked off with angle irons to ensure that visitors cannot enter.

4.13.
Peering into the mine at Graphite (pictured in fig. 4.12); it is a steady 54 degrees Fahrenheit inside the mine, and blasts of cool air are constantly blowing out through this opening.

4.14. **Facing page**
The remains of the crushing mill at Graphite in 2017. The two columns read: "FEB 1917" and "APRIL 24, 1917."

4.15. ◀
One of the cellar holes from the abandoned workers' village at Graphite in 2017.

4.16. ▼
The remains of a stairway at Graphite with a tree growing out of the top step.

Adirondack Charcoal Kilns and Lime Kilns

There is probably no way of knowing exactly how many charcoal kilns and lime kilns were once scattered throughout the Adirondacks, but charcoal in enormous quantities was needed in the production of iron, and lime was the primary ingredient in mortar. Hundreds of these relatively short-term kilns were no doubt in operation in the Adirondacks, but few have received serious documentation in the field, except in the adjacent state of Vermont (Rolando 1992). Still, it is not unusual for archeologists to be called in to examine the remains of these structures, and I especially remember being asked to look at the stone foundation of what was probably a kiln in the town of Keene in 2010 (fig. 4.17). Bricks from the fallen superstructure were scattered everywhere, but there were no clear indicators on the ground surface of what had been processed there. Sadly, all I could do was give the property owner a list of possibilities.

Even though short-term industrial structures can be hard to identify and are often neglected by scholars, an excellent project was conducted by the New York State Museum between the summer of 2013 and the spring of 2014 at the site of a lime kiln just south of the Million Dollar Beach in Lake George. This had been constructed from the local limestone, which is abundant there, and the kiln was found completely buried under rubble. Ovoid in shape, it measured 3.9 meters (12 ¾ feet) by 3 meters (10 feet) and had walls that were about 1 meter thick. It had been well hidden since the time of the French and

4.17.
A collapsed kiln base in Keene (2010), about 8 feet long by 5 feet wide.

4.18.
The surface of a
lime kiln in the
Lake George Battle-
field Park, partially
exposed in 2014.

Indian War and was most likely a kiln constructed by the "Jersey Blues" militia (the First New Jersey Regiment) when they were encamped at the south end of Lake George in 1759. The artifacts found in and around the kiln included hand-wrought nails, bottle glass, tobacco pipe fragments, a .69 caliber lead musket ball, and, of course, bits of charcoal.

The early British military encampments at the south end of Lake George needed an ample supply of lime, especially once construction of Fort George began. In the summer of 2014, a field school from SUNY Adirondack partially cleared the surface of a second lime kiln a short distance away—in the Lake George Battlefield Park—and within five hundred feet of the ruins of Fort George (fig. 4.18). This second kiln most likely supplied lime for mortar that went into creating the surviving bastion of Fort George. No artifacts were found, but it was exciting to have found a second kiln site so close to the first.

Adirondack Tanneries

The rise of tanneries had an enormous impact on the settlement of the Adirondacks, as the processing of animal hides into usable leather caused towns to spring up in remote areas. By the mid-1800s, tanneries operated in almost every town in the Adirondacks, and exceptionally large quantities of bark from the eastern hemlock (*Tsuga canadensis*) were used in the tanning of hides. Consequently it was necessary for tanneries to be built close to hemlock stands. The actual tanning involved soaking the hides in vats of tannic acid derived from the hemlock bark, which gave the leather a deep, reddish-brown color.

4.19. ▶
A stack of hemlock bark on display in the Adirondack Experience as part of its exhibit on the tanning industry.

4.20. ▼
Part of the foundation of the Alpine Tannery in Minerva that operated from 1847 to 1867. This was photographed in 2017.

Tanneries required hard physical labor and noxious substances, and increasingly streams were polluted. Arguably no other industry in the Adirondacks was as smelly and harmful to the environment. While the Adirondacks had 153 tanneries in 1850, by 1880 there were only 112, and the remaining tanneries were rapidly closing (McMartin 1891). By the end of the nineteenth century, the tanning industry was essentially gone, and vast stands of hemlock had been decimated. Fortunately the hemlock has gradually grown back since then, and exhibits on the tanning industry may be found in the Adirondack Experience on Blue Mountain Lake (fig. 4.19).

While the ruins of tanneries survive as archeological sites in a great many Adirondack towns (fig. 4.20), archeologists have rarely shown an interest in excavating them. In fact, given the pollutants and the smells emerging from the tanning vats, these sites will probably remain undisturbed for a long time to come!

Adirondack Timber Industry and Sawmills

The timber industry in the Adirondacks has been important ever since the first Europeans entered the region in the seventeenth century and began harvesting the forests. The historical literature describing this industry is extensive, and it has been observed that lumbering, the tanning industry, the paper industry, and the charcoal industry all resulted in much destruction of the woodlands and consequent erosion. Gradually, with urging by early environmentalists such as the topographical engineer Verplanck Colvin, a bill creating the Adirondack Park passed the New York State Legislature in 1892, and a "blue line" identified those areas where state acquisition of private land was to be concentrated. Soon after, in 1895, the state-owned lands within the Adirondack Park were designated, in an amendment to the New York State Constitution, as "forever wild." From this beginning, the mix of public and private lands within the Adirondack Park has received a significant level of protection that has continued down to the present day.

These are popular, much-discussed themes, but to an archeologist there is also an interest in the logging camps, sawmills, pulp mills, and all other physical traces of the timber industry that was, and still is, so vital to people who reside in this region. While logging in the Adirondacks has been described in detail in historical sources (e.g., Fox 1901; Hochschild 1962b; Keller 1980; Donaldson 1996), there has not been a comparable body of literature describing what has physically survived on the ground, with one very recent exception. In a ground-breaking study, the "transition from extractive enterprises to renewable energy" along streams in the northern Adirondacks has been demonstrated by looking at the archeological remains of some of the dams, power canals, penstocks, and mills that have survived at several industrial sites (Quiggle and Kirk 2015). We clearly need more studies of this type, and hopefully archeologists will also begin to research camp life, examining such topics as building construction techniques, the trash discarded by loggers, the sourcing of manufactured goods in the camps, and the evidence for leisure or nonwork activities (for example, evidence for religious life in the camps).

The Adirondack Experience on Blue Mountain Lake is one of the few places where these stories are told in detail, with extensive exhibits on such themes as "Log Drives," "Log Jams," and "Camp Construction" (fig. 4.21), and with displays showing some of the artifacts that might be found if camp dumps were to be excavated (fig. 4.22). While archeology has not yet played a major role in researching survivals from the timber industry, it will most assuredly be needed in the years ahead.

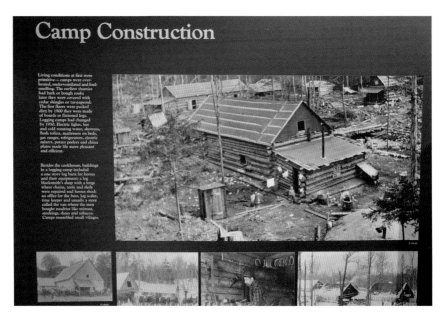

4.21.

What is now the Adirondack Park was once covered with hundreds of logging operations, now reduced to ruins. This exhibit in the Adirondack Experience illustrating camp construction gives an excellent sense of the structural remains that archeologists might hope to find.

4.22.

This exhibit in the Adirondack Experience displays the kinds of artifacts—in this case medicine bottles—that no doubt will be found by archeologists when we begin to dig the sites of logging camps.

Adirondack Bridges

Industrial archeologists love studying historic bridges, and the Adirondacks have an abundance of these. The Ausable River alone is traversed by some seventeen bridges that are listed on the National Register of Historic Places, and one of these is a covered bridge in the town of Jay. While traditional archeologists cannot "dig up" a bridge, industrial archeologists document standing bridges and have found that the Adirondacks contain numerous stringer bridges and exhibit a variety of truss designs (fig. 4.23). All these bridge types occasionally face danger from storms and flooding, and thus aboveground documentation of every historic bridge is needed.

Adirondack Railroads

Railroads, railroad stations, and tracks have many fans within the industrial archeology community, and the Adirondacks have a great many abandoned lines and stations, as well as a few railroad lines that still operate today (fig. 4.24) (Hochschild 1962a; Kudish 1985, 1996; Johnson 2009). Railways were heavily used in the Adirondacks from about 1871 until the 1930s, for the transport of both passengers and freight, but then automobiles increasingly replaced the trains. Today the Saratoga and North Creek Railway and the Upper Hudson River Railroad scenic railway are good examples of the so-called "tourist trains" that are fighting to stay alive, even though car culture now typifies the Adirondacks.

4.23. ▲
The Hadley Bow Bridge (Hadley Parabolic Bridge) that crosses the Sacandaga River is an excellent representative of the many early bridges that survive throughout the Adirondacks. It is an iron bridge built by the Berlin Iron Bridge Company in 1885 and is the only surviving iron semi-deck lenticular truss bridge in New York State. This photograph shows the bridge after restoration and re-opening in 2006.

4.24.
The railroad in Hadley passing over the Sacandaga River.

4.25.
The North Creek Railroad Station in 2017. The station was built in 1874, and this was where Theodore Roosevelt caught the train after the assassination of President William McKinley in September 1901. The station is currently operated as the northern terminus of the Saratoga and North Creek Railway, which features ski trains and summer service south to Saratoga Springs.

For visitors, railroad stations are the most visible reminders of the earlier dependency on railroads, and easily the best-known of the stations is the North Creek Railroad Station where Theodore Roosevelt caught the train after the assassination of President William McKinley (fig. 4.25). However, there are plenty of other, attractive stations scattered along rail lines throughout the region (fig. 4.26), and these are popular tourist attractions.

Final Thoughts

Industrial archeology has a promising future in the Adirondack Mountains, and we need to view these many industrial sites as a wonderful research opportunity for students and scholars. The quality and variety of industrial ruins,

4.26.
The Riverside (Riparius) Train Station in 2017. Built in 1913, it is currently operated as a station for the Upper Hudson River Railroad scenic railway.

coupled with a very high retention rate, suggest that nearly all these sites will remain undisturbed for a long time to come. The remains of extractive industries and logging camps are especially abundant and should provide scholars with many opportunities for research into how early industrial processes were performed. Also, the associated abandoned towns — ghost towns — once occupied by workers of diverse ethnic backgrounds have enormous potential for studies into labor history. Loggers and miners led difficult lives here, often far removed from their families, and yet the Adirondacks provided them with employment and a home in a truly beautiful wilderness setting. Of course, these earlier denizens of the Adirondacks would no doubt find it amazing that modern visitors to the area are almost always fascinated by the things they left behind.

5.1.
The Starbuck Farm in Chestertown, with the Adirondack Mountains rising in the background. This aerial photograph was taken in the 1950s, showing one cluster of outbuildings around the farmhouse in the lower left, and a separate cluster of large barns in the upper right. (North is at the top.) Since this picture was taken, the longest building (a chicken house) has been removed, along with the shed behind it and also the woodshed that was attached to the farmhouse.

FAMILY FARMS AND THE RURAL LANDSCAPE

I have always believed that there could be nothing more boring to dig up than an old farm. That may be because I was born into what was then the only active farm family in a small town, and in school I would be teased by my classmates ("You farmer you") to the point where I couldn't leave home fast enough. Still, I always assumed that someday, when I was too old and decrepit to go on digs anymore, I would probably have to dodder home to dig in the garden behind the farmhouse where I grew up (fig. 5.1). Maybe I would find a few pottery sherds and some tines from old rakes, and admittedly that doesn't sound very exciting.

That is not to say that I have never dug a farm site. I have, plenty of times, in New Hampshire and Scotland, and other historical archeologists have dug up the remains of farms all over the world. A useful compendium of relevant articles on this topic may be found in volumes 30 and 31 of the journal *Northeast Historical Archaeology*, which covers nineteenth-century farm excavations throughout the northeastern United States. Also, the *Annual Proceedings of the Dublin Seminar for New England Folklife* for 1986 was devoted to "the Farm" and presented a wonderful array of articles about farm life and material culture (Benes 1988). But really. Dig up a farm, when there are temples and pyramids out there? It has taken me many years to realize that my indifference toward farms was wrong, and I would like to give some of the reasons why.

Part of the explanation for my lifelong ambivalence toward farmstead archeology is that traditional farming was never very successful in the Adirondacks. There was a time when subsistence farms dotted much of what is now the Adirondack Park — after all, land was cheap in the late eighteenth and early nineteenth centuries — but soils everywhere were thin and rocky, markets were far away, and transportation was difficult on the poor roads. Farmers soon moved west in search of better farmland, or else their offspring shifted into other professions. Still, some families managed to achieve success with hop growing, beekeeping, berry picking, maple sugaring, potato farming, and apple growing. Not unexpectedly, apple cider has always been a popular product of the Adirondacks, and my family put our cider presses to work every fall, squeezing the lower-grade apples.

The Starbuck family was fairly representative of this subsistence pattern, and my ancestors were always highly diversified — they eked out a living from a little bit of everything. Flocks of sheep covered our fields in the nineteenth century, and by the time of my father's generation, the focus had become beef and dairy cows, white leghorn chickens (for their eggs), and some corn, apples, and tomatoes that were sold to local summer resorts. Only later did Christmas tree farming take over, with trees being one of the few successful "crops" in a region that has a fairly short growing season. (Most crops in the Adirondacks must mature in ninety days or less.) In the case of the Starbuck Farm, we began planting Scotch pine Christmas trees in 1956, and that ultimately proved fairly successful.

Very few farms in the Adirondacks have been studied by archeologists, and so it has been with considerable interest that Adirondackers have witnessed excavations by Professor Hadley Kruczek-Aaron and her students from SUNY Potsdam at the site of Timbuctoo in North Elba (the John Brown Farm State Historic Site), an experimental free black settlement. It was here in the fall of 1846 that the abolitionist Gerrit Smith planned to endow three thousand grantees with plots of land, forty acres each, that he hoped would bring them the right to vote in New York State. This was definitely a fascinating social experiment, but most of the participants had come from various New York cities and knew little about farming. In fact, very few had the means to move here and actually cultivate the land. Only about two hundred settled on the forty-acre parcels, and the North Elba farming settlement had been declared a failure by 1855. The "Timbuctoo Archaeology Project," as the Potsdam effort is known, conducted digs in 2010, 2013, 2015, and 2017, and Kruczek-Aaron is hoping to learn more about the daily lives of the Timbuctoo settlers.

Archeology at the Starbuck Farm

One of the few Adirondack farms that actually has seen archeology is, in fact, my own family's farm (Starbuck 2009). (I decided *not* to wait until my old age before beginning excavations at the farm.) Farming was the mainstay of the early Quaker families — the Starbucks, the Leggetts, and others — that founded Chestertown in the 1790s. The earliest settlers in this Warren County community raised wheat, corn, potatoes, sheep, pigs, and cows, and agriculture was soon accompanied by tanneries, sawmills, and various forest-related industries that lasted throughout the nineteenth and into the twentieth century. The tannery long owned by Charles Faxon became the business that Chestertown is best remembered for, and sole leather, cured leather, shoes, boots, and board lumber were some of the principal products of the town.

Chestertown has inevitably changed a great deal over the years since then, and it is now a scenic retirement community and the home of Lincoln Logs, the construction company Peckham Industries, a recently opened medical

5.2.
Historical view of
the Starbuck farm-
house on July 4,
1916. Pictured are
Bert and Carrie
(Leggett) Starbuck,
rear, and Robert and
Samuel Starbuck.

marijuana dispensary, and a variety of restaurants and small businesses. However, a part of Chestertown that has changed very little in more than two
centuries is the Starbuck Farm, home to six generations of Starbucks who
originally arrived from the town of Easton in Washington County. The family
line dates back to whalers who lived on Nantucket, and a branch of the family
briefly operated out of the whaling port of Hudson, New York, before pushing
on to Easton. The end of hostilities after the American Revolution prompted
the Starbucks and numerous others to move still farther north, thus becoming
Adirondackers before the close of the eighteenth century. While most of the
Starbucks had been mariners in the years leading up to their arrival in Chestertown, farming nevertheless became the livelihood for at least one member
of every generation that followed.

Many Starbuck farm buildings have come and gone since the 1790s when
my ancestors built and briefly occupied a log cabin somewhere close by. What
survives today in Chestertown is a central core of buildings — the original
circa 1800 farmhouse (fig. 5.2) and six early outbuildings, accompanied by
two recent garages, a pole barn, and two observatories, resting on a landscape
that includes 401 acres of fields, pine and spruce forest, logging roads, farm
ponds, and fences and stone walls (fig. 5.3). Some of the areas that are forested
today were formerly cleared fields, used for grazing sheep in the nineteenth
century but subsequently allowed to return to forest. Today the farm is divided
into approximately 60 acres of open fields surrounded by roughly 340 acres
of forest. The integrity of the farm landscape has been maintained since its
original settlement, and this complements the integrity of the buildings. All
in all, this is an unusually intact representative of the early days of farming

5.3.
A second aerial
photograph of the
Starbuck Farm
taken in the 1950s.
(West is at the top.)
In this view, the
farmhouse stands
out more clearly in
the center of the
picture.

in the Adirondacks, and in 1993 the Starbuck Farm was certified by the New York State Agricultural Society as the first New York Century Farm in Warren County.

The Starbuck farm buildings were always repaired conservatively, using recycled materials from earlier buildings whenever possible, and the preservation issues confronting this historic farm are considerable. However, for anyone who has grown up close to the land, Adirondack farm memories and "roots" are strong, and after years of living and practicing archeology elsewhere, I returned to the family farm after my father died in 2002, to oversee the restoration effort. The preservation questions are often difficult to answer: What should be saved and restored? Does anything need to be torn down? Should the farm be interpreted and restored to a particular time period? Are there earlier farm activities that should be brought back to life, and what new farm industries might be introduced to give the farm a viable future? Above all, how can the preservation and restoration of an Adirondack farm be achieved in a fashion that is most respectful to a family's long-standing traditions of independence, frugality, and moderation? Clearly these are concerns faced by every owner of an old Adirondack farm, and retaining a sense of place and preserving memory are the ultimate measures of success in the preservation field. What is at stake is the very heart and soul of a family farm, both its past and its future.

Even today most communities have at least a few intact early farms — both the buildings and surrounding fields — although subsistence farming has largely been supplanted by more specialized organic farms, berry farms, or orchards. The continuing loss of the region's farms and farm buildings has been tragic, but barns and other outbuildings were never intended to last forever, and the cost of restoration or reconstruction is considerable. What is the best solution? How do property owners decide whether to restore or demolish their historic farm buildings? Many factors feed into the decision-making process, including cost, family history and tradition, current and projected uses, possible tax breaks, and the ever-evolving standards of the historic preservation movement.

Few if any systematic records have been kept of the remains of early farm buildings in the Adirondacks, but clearly there are fewer and fewer farm landscapes that have retained their integrity. The Starbuck Farm has resisted this trend, although within just the past forty-five years it has lost its sugarhouse, icehouse, woodshed, hired man's house, several chicken houses, and its privy house (a "three-holer" that was attached to the side of the woodshed). Still, some of the most important buildings have survived, including the farmhouse (ca. 1800 for the core; it was later expanded ca. 1840–1850); the cow barn (ca. 1800 for the core); the sheep (or east) barn (ca. 1800); a later horse barn (ca. 1840), which reflects the growing affluence and sophistication of the early Victorian period; the corn house (ca. 1800); the hog house (ca. 1800, but with later modifications); and a calf shed (ca. 1800), made up of recycled pieces from several other farm buildings. As some of these buildings suggest, the Starbuck Farm at various times throughout its history produced wool, beef, pork, logs, firewood, maple syrup, honey, and eggs, and the farm made yet another transition in the mid-twentieth century, when it became the setting for a Christmas tree plantation.

My brother James and I played and worked in every one of these buildings while growing up, carving our initials (JS and DS) onto the exterior of the corn house, next to the initials of our father and his brother (SS and RS) from a generation before (fig. 5.4). At various times I painted all the barns, stacked sap buckets in the corn house, dug utility ditches in the fields, chased pigs around the hog house, and was sneaky enough to carve everyone else's initials (not mine!) onto the interior walls of the three-holer. I even remember how as a teenager, before I decided to become an archeologist, I occasionally looked underneath the horse barn, where I could see an intact bitters bottle lying in the crawl space. I didn't know at the time what "bitters" were, but I remember wondering whether it had alcohol in it. (It does, along with herbs and citrus flavoring.)

However, it takes more than fond memories to preserve a farm. With the passing of my brother in 2007, it became clear that the restoration of the farm could not be delayed any longer. Buildings on the farm are of post-and-beam

5.4.

Initials on the exterior of the Starbuck corn house: the initials RS (Robert Starbuck) and SS (Samuel Starbuck) appear on the left, carved nearly a century ago; and the initials JS (James Starbuck) and DS (David Starbuck) appear on the right, carved about fifty years ago. (The "JS" initials were long ago carved over, no doubt by the younger brother with the initials "DS.")

construction, typical of eighteenth- and nineteenth-century buildings, and these were on the verge of collapse. Nostalgia had to be replaced by historic preservation, commencing with the buildings that were in "crisis mode," teetering on their dry-laid-stone foundations. Restoration work on the corn house began in November 2007, followed by the horse barn in September 2008, and then by virtually every other building at the farm. Preservation professionals, along with timber framers, carpenters, electricians, and plumbers, have replaced or repaired foundations, siding, and roofs across the entire farm, and modern electrical and plumbing systems have been installed whenever necessary.

The farm has experienced a long-overdue resurrection. Perhaps most important, much of the wood used in the restoration (chiefly pine and hemlock) was harvested from the farm itself by loggers Martin Cooper and Billy MacGlashan, with modern Starbuck wood (of the same species as the original timbers) being used to supplement and replace the historic wood. Admittedly visitors have sometimes asked, "Why don't you tear the old buildings down and start over? Wouldn't that be cheaper?" But a key goal of the restoration effort is to ensure that this is still "the Starbuck Farm" and not simply new buildings erected on the footprints of the original buildings.

Restoration, however, does not just involve the work of skilled craftsmen as they stabilize and repair weathered buildings. Beginning in the fall of 2007, when the floor and subfloor of the corn house were lifted as a prelude

5.5.
Part of the dump underneath the Starbuck corn house.

to replacing rotted joists, a rich layer of late nineteenth-century artifacts was discovered in the crawl space underneath the floor (fig. 5.5). From that time forward, archeology has been an essential part of the preservation process in restoring the farm. Archeology has been conducted underneath virtually every one of the historic buildings, and even the timber framers and carpenters have helped to save every last piece of pottery or glass that they encounter under the floors of buildings.

Hidden underneath the corn house were dozens of shoes, hundreds of pieces of leather from the manufacture of shoes, intact medicine bottles, ceramics (chamber pots, plates, cups, stoneware crocks and jugs), taps for sugar maple trees, corncobs, butchered bones, enamelware, Ball jars for canning, several scythe blades, sleigh bells, and much more. All had been thrown into an enormous dump, occupying the crawl space under the building and hidden from view, but just waiting to be interpreted. What insights might they reveal into the behavior of past generations of the Starbuck family? (My ancestors!) Were they the ultra-straitlaced farmers that my parents had described so often, who never took a drink and never smoked, and who never spent a cent if they didn't have to? To an archeologist, it is the artifacts cast into dumps, cellar holes, crawl spaces, privies, and yards that reveal the consumption patterns of Adirondack families. Would I find evidence for alcohol, tobacco, fancy dishes, and "nonessential" items? Were these farmers living prosperous lives, or were they just getting by? After a lifetime of believing that excavating

5.6. ▲
A few of the shoes and pieces for making shoes discovered underneath the floor of the Starbuck corn house.

5.7. ▶
A wood shoe last found underneath the corn house.

a nineteenth-century farm might not be very exciting, I suddenly faced the pleasant prospect of using archeology as an essential first step toward the preservation of my own family's historic farm. Farmstead archeology had never looked this interesting before!

We found many shoe fragments, strips of leather, and shoe lasts (forms used in the manufacture of shoes) underneath the corn house, suggesting that my ancestors had probably been repairing or assembling shoes during the winter months when there was no farming to be done. This activity had never been mentioned in my family's oral traditions (figs. 5.6 and 5.7). One possibility, of course, is that these came from the shoe manufacturing business that had been started by Isaac Starbuck only a few miles away in what has long been known as "Starbuckville" (*Adirondack Journal*, June 8, 2013, 10). Receiving shoe parts from a close relative, and assembling them during slow times of the year (before Isaac's business burned down in 1870), would seem quite reasonable.

5.8.
Linda White excavating under the floor of the Starbuck horse barn in the fall of 2008.

Just as surprising was the discovery of several reed-plates from Hohner harmonicas under the floor of the corn house, somewhat at odds with a family that has no musical aptitude whatever! Much of what we found matched the contents of Sears, Roebuck or Montgomery Ward catalogs printed in the late 1800s, the nearly universal sources of dry goods for those who lived on farms in the countryside.

Just a few feet north of the corn house is the horse barn, the most modern of the farm's traditional outbuildings. When the barn floor was raised to replace the joists, it too revealed a dumping ground for those prepared to throw trash or broken tools into the crawl space, or who were too lazy to carry their trash to the many farm dumps in the more distant woods (fig. 5.8). Dozens of embossed medicine and liniment bottles lay there, revealing the various local druggists who had supplied questionable cures to my ancestors or to the animals at the farm. The inscriptions on the bottles included "Hall's Balsam for the Lungs, John F. Henry & Co. New York," "Sanford & Pearsall Pharmacists, Glens Falls & Chestertown NY," "George W. Sisson Druggist, Glens Falls N.Y.," "Rev. NH Downs Vegetable Balsamic Elixir," and "Compound Extract of Sarsaparilla."

I was especially eager to discover whether the bitters bottle was still there, the one that I had first seen when I peered under the barn over fifty years ago. It was! In fact, we found several bitters bottles under the horse barn, and one was embossed with the words "DR. J. HOSTETTER'S STOMACH BITTERS" and another with "JOHNSON'S CALISAYA BITTERS" and "BURLINGTON VT" (fig. 5.9). These bottles were buried beneath about six inches of hay and dirt that

5.9.
Two of the bitters bottles found underneath the horse barn at the Starbuck Farm. The lower bottle reads "JOHNSON'S CALISAYA BITTERS."

had sifted through cracks in the barn floor in the years since I was a teenager. There was a single wine bottle and one clear flask that may have been for whiskey, but otherwise the reputation of my ancestors as teetotalers has held up quite well. Still, as with most other Americans in the nineteenth century, the Starbucks loved experimenting with patent medicines, and these invariably contained a healthy supply of alcohol.

The artifacts under the horse barn included several inkwells (fig. 5.10), doorknobs, hand tools, doll parts, a glass egg (placed in nests to encourage chickens to lay eggs), many buttons, pen knives, tobacco pipes, and — quite surprisingly — two small Staffordshire cats (fig. 5.11). Broken glass and pottery (chiefly stoneware, whiteware, and yellowware) lay everywhere (fig. 5.12), as well as cut and wire nails that are helpful in dating buildings. One of the worn tobacco pipes had the mysterious initials "JP" carved into the bowl (fig. 5.13), a find made even more curious because it was discovered underneath the barn by one of the timber framers I had hired, "Joseph Perreault." (No, he insisted, he had not been the one to carve the initials.)

Archeology was also conducted under and around the exterior of the hog house (fig. 5.14), where we found a complete pig's foot, as well as pig hair just about everywhere. Perhaps more unexpectedly, inside the building's cast iron stove we found hundreds of bone fragments from pigs. Their bones had been burned as part of the fuel when pig heads were rendered in the cauldron atop the stove, a "CALDRON FURNACE" manufactured by "SYRACUSE STOVE WORKS SYRACUSE, N.Y." Fragments of window glass were discovered under an outer wall of the hog house, revealing where a window had been removed long ago, to be replaced by a solid wall. In small ways such as this, archeology is demonstrating that artifact recovery and interpretation needs to be an integral research tool during the restoration of every farm building.

5.10. ▲▲
Some of the inkwells discovered underneath the horse barn.

5.11. ▲
Staffordshire cats discovered underneath the horse barn.

5.12. ▲▶
Reconstructed vessels of stoneware, whiteware, and yellowware from the horse barn excavation.

5.13. ▶
Tobacco pipes discovered underneath the horse barn. The pipe with the initials "JP" is in the center of the top row.

5.14.
The eastern side of
the Starbuck hog
house, just before
the start of resto-
ration in 2009.

After architectural restoration and archeology were completed at the corn
house, horse barn, and hog house — all positioned side by side at the southern
end of the farm, close to the farmhouse — we went on to tackle the three
much-larger barns clustered together about five hundred feet to the north.
These are the cow barn, the sheep (east) barn, and the calf shed (fig. 5.15), and
once again we replaced timbers, siding, and roofing that was rotted while seeking to preserve as much original fabric as possible. Also, twentieth-century gal-
vanized roofs (with cedar shakes underneath) were replaced by wood shingles.
The recovery of artifacts underneath the floors of these buildings was again
a very high priority, but here an interesting pattern emerged. Large numbers
of domestic, people-oriented artifacts had been recovered from the outbuildings closest to the farmhouse, but the more distant barns lacked all personal
artifacts and instead contained pulleys, grain scoops, liniment bottles for the
farm animals, and pieces from rakes and shovels. These were perhaps not as
informative about the consumption practices of a farm family, but nevertheless
they reflected the work activities conducted on a typical Adirondack farm.

Some Final Thoughts on the Archeology of Farming

Literally thousands of artifacts have been recovered at the Starbuck Farm and
subsequently processed and identified by my students in the Archeology Laboratory at Plymouth State University. I am reminded of some of the famous
archeologists who acquired or owned the sites they dug, especially General
Augustus Pitt-Rivers at Cranborne Chase in England and Sir Arthur Evans

5.15.
The northern cluster of Starbuck barns: (*left to right*) the calf shed, cow barn, and sheep (east) barn as they appear today. At the far right, a pole barn was erected in 2016 to display historic farm equipment.

at Knossos on Crete. Still, never did I anticipate that archeology would play a significant role in interpreting my own family's Adirondack farm. Perhaps "archeology begins at home" is the best rubric in this case.

Modern archeology invariably seeks to tell the stories of those who have been ignored by history or who were so busy that they had no time to put the events of their lives down on paper. The remains of many hundreds of abandoned farms are spread all across the Adirondacks, and they will provide rich excavation opportunities for future generations of archeologists. Now that I have finally discovered that farmstead archeology can be truly interesting, I have no doubt that this will also become the perspective of the archeologists who come after me.

In exploring the Starbuck Farm, I would argue that Adirondack farmers have left behind a legacy of artifacts that provide insights into commerce, mass consumerism, exchange networks, and even mild "vices" (tobacco and alcohol). Architectural artifacts can help to date buildings, and domestic artifacts reveal changing technologies, sources of supply, and personal preferences. Bitters bottles, inkwells, and locally made shoes have long passed away, and yet here they lie underneath farm buildings.

Most important for me, farmstead archeology is able to provide a very deep and emotional connection to my own ancestors, and I often find myself wondering who purchased, used, broke, and then discarded a particular artifact. I especially would like to decipher *which* ancestor threw all those bitters bottles under the horse barn! My ultimate goal, though, is to find the original Starbuck log cabin that was erected in 1794 or 1795, predating the still-standing farm buildings of circa 1800. Now *that* is something I would truly love to dig up in my old age, when I'm no longer able to travel to faraway ruins!

6.1.
Frontier Town as it appears today just off Exit 29 of the Adirondack Northway (I-87).

TOURISM AND THE HOSPITALITY INDUSTRY

Communities in the Adirondack Park welcome hundreds of thousands of visitors each year, many looking for opportunities to hike in the region's mountains, or to canoe on the many lakes and rivers, or to ski at one of the popular ski resorts, such as Whiteface Mountain or Gore Mountain, or perhaps to visit the Adirondack Experience on Blue Mountain Lake. For visitors from New York City, Long Island, or New Jersey, camping and touring in the Adirondacks is a godsend, a way to enjoy a peaceful getaway from the hustle and bustle of urban life.

These activities have left behind a great many historic sites and traces that have seen very little archeology. Still, the ruins of hotels, campgrounds, amusement parks, and ski areas are worth a closer look, especially by hikers who enjoy viewing signs of the past on the surface of the ground. Who isn't curious about what life used to be like in the Adirondacks? While some may view abandoned hospitality and tourism sites as eyesores that need to be "cleaned up," to an archeologist these ruins provide a wonderful opportunity to study the habits of past visitors.

Outstanding examples of this are abandoned theme parks, such as Frontier Town in North Hudson, about one hundred miles north of Albany (fig. 6.1). Frontier Town opened to the public as a Wild West theme park on July 4, 1952, and provided a you-are-there western experience to families who enjoyed viewing an attempted stagecoach robbery, a steam train that was ambushed by robbers, demonstrations of the Pony Express, a rodeo twice a day, a replica Indian village, a fort, log cabins, a grain mill, animal pens, and various storefronts (fig. 6.2). During its heyday in the 1960s and '70s, this 267-acre property was an exciting memorial to the vanished American West. I remember visiting there with my classmates as a boy and watching the stagecoach race into town, chased by robbers on horseback, and then the shootout that followed. Afterward, I saw one of the robbers tied up and punished by "dunking" him into a pond, and then I looked for some frontier-related mementos that I could buy before returning home.

These memories are probably shared by every other child who grew up in the Adirondacks at that time, and Frontier Town was immensely popular until it closed in 1998. Today its remaining, dilapidated buildings do rather look like survivals from the early West (fig. 6.3) (Bramen 2016). Unfortunately, this

6.2.
A postcard view of
Frontier Town at its
height.

abandoned western theme park is now frequently mentioned in local newspapers as an eyesore that needs to be sold, or removed, or at least somehow be made to generate income once again. On a far more positive note, Governor Andrew Cuomo has proposed that this site become a new recreational gateway into the Adirondacks (*Glens Falls Post-Star*, Jan. 13, 2017, B1, B7). Some of the old theme park features are still there, including a covered bridge and the mill. However, as an archeologist, I see the ruins as a great opportunity to do some digging and to learn more about what Adirondack tourists were consuming and experiencing from the 1950s through the 1990s. What souvenirs did they leave behind? Candy wrappers? Empty soda bottles? Maybe there are clusters of blank gun cartridges that would show just where the shootouts took place. A theme park with thousands of annual visitors also means thousands of twentieth-century artifacts lying just beneath the surface. Hopefully future archeologists will have a chance to investigate this.

There are other theme parks that have not closed but have simply changed their primary function. Storytown U.S.A., on the southern edge of the Adirondack Park in Queensbury, opened on June 26, 1954, and it told a host of nursery-rhyme stories to children (and their parents) on a small, five-acre parcel. "Children could feed the three little pigs, meet Mary and her little lamb and crawl into the old woman's shoe and the house that Jack built" (Hagerty 2014). The creation of Storytown by Charles R. Wood even predated the opening of Disneyland in Florida! The remnants of Storytown have long since been expanded and built over to become a modern, 140-acre theme park. It was

6.3.
One of the many fallen-down buildings at Frontier Town in June 2017. This really is one of the early stages in the formation of an archeological site. Abandonment is followed by vandalism, and then the roof falls in, and in time only the foundation stones will be left.

renamed the Great Escape Fun Park in 1983 and today bills itself as the Great Escape and Splashwater Kingdom. While now best known for its amusement rides (it is a Six Flags theme park), archeological artifacts no doubt lie under the surface of the ground from the days of Little Miss Muffet, Little Boy Blue, and Alice in Wonderland. I was one of the many children who often visited Storytown U.S.A., and perhaps I might find an artifact or two from when I was there in the fourth grade!

What about abandoned ski areas? The remains of lifts, car engines, and rope tows are scattered throughout mountainous areas, and written histories have been prepared for nearly seven hundred lost ski areas across the Adirondack Mountains, the Green Mountains of Vermont, and the White Mountains of New Hampshire (Jeremy Davis, personal communication, Dec. 2, 2016). Most ski operations were very small, and many of them consisted of just a rope tow and an open slope. (The very first rope tow was Schaefer Tow at Over the Ridge Slopes in North Creek, operated from 1935 to 1936.) Many of the trails were cut in the 1930s by ski clubs and by the Civilian Conservation Corps. Jeremy Davis has conducted a tremendous amount of historical research and surface documentation while recording these abandoned ski areas, most of which are grown over with forest today (Davis 2012, 2014). Perhaps what is most amazing is that so much of the equipment is still hidden in the woods, at the top of former ski slopes, where it can easily be visited. For example, the operation at Blister Hill in Warrensburg was torched in 1978, but its engine is still resting there, only two minutes from the nearest parking lot (fig. 6.4).

6.4.
An abandoned ski engine on Blister Hill in Warrensburg in 2016.

Modern-day environmental regulations would no doubt make it extremely difficult to walk away from so much equipment, but early ski area proprietors often simply abandoned their equipment when their businesses closed.

The presence of tourists in the Adirondacks can be documented in other ways. In the early 1970s, a new type of research began at the University of Arizona, and it has been identified as the "Garbage Project" ever since. For archeologists reared on dreams of discovering "the very old" and "the very far away," it had now become fashionable to document the very recent artifacts of our own culture. The students of William Rathje, a University of Arizona professor, collected bags of garbage from the Tucson city dump, quantitatively analyzing the trash of modern Americans (Rathje 1974; Rathje and Murphy 2001). Sometimes termed "garbology," this new type of archeology spread across the United States, the goal of every study being to use modern trash to discover what Americans *actually* threw out, comparing artifacts in the dumps with what informants *claimed* to have consumed and discarded (using oral and written surveys). While no garbage project per se has been conducted in the Adirondacks, our work in Lake George Village — one of the premier tourist destinations in the United States — has inevitably included the saving of "tourist artifacts" from every spot where we have excavated.

A fascinating example of this was when we dug the 1756 well at Fort William Henry in 1997, recovering literally thousands of coins thrown in by tourists since the 1950s, along with thousands of wads of chewing gum, sheriff's badges, sunglasses, bottle caps, and pull tabs (Starbuck 2001, 2002b). While my students may sometimes have believed their dig director was slightly nuts for saving such recent artifacts, I never questioned that we needed to record the vestiges of the visitors who come each summer to Lake George. Over the long haul, the stories of visitors in the 1950s and later are just as important as the stories of soldiers who fought there in the 1750s or Native Americans who fished there thousands of years before. Sometimes it is even possible to identify the exact source of some of the recent artifacts. Several years ago, at the conclusion of an archeology conference, a fellow archeologist — Tim Abel — came up to me and said, "You know that Batman figure [about three inches tall] that you found in the well at Fort William Henry? Well, I wanted you to know that it was my son that threw it into the well." It truly is a very small world for archeologists who deal with the recent past.

We practice this same diligence at every dig site in Lake George, and over the years that we have excavated in the Lake George Battlefield Park (2000–2001 and 2014–2016) we have saved every bottle, aluminum can, pull tab, cork, bottle cap, pen, pencil, button, film can, or cigarette butt that lies on the surface or is buried in the ground. They are the artifacts of our own culture, and they tell the story of what twentieth- and twenty-first-century visitors brought with them into the park. Besides, if we ever want to know whether more visitors to Lake George were Coke drinkers versus Pepsi drinkers, we will have the data to answer that question!

Will the artifacts left behind by contemporary visitors to the Battlefield Park ever command the respect and public interest that attend the discovery of musket balls and projectile points? That is extremely hard to answer, but we archeologists keep expanding our subject matter. Personally, I have little doubt that everything we leave behind in Lake George today — whether thrown into a well, dropped next to an outdoor grill, or left on the sidewalk — will eventually be subjected to rigorous archeological analysis. Archeologists are just a little bit obsessive-compulsive about saving everything, and the artifacts of tourism have stories to tell.

The Excavation of a B&B

Chestertown may be the quintessential Adirondack village: small, proud of its traditions, occupied by a mix of old families and new, and fated to lose most of its young people to jobs in the cities. I grew up there in the 1950s and '60s, finally returning in 1998, just as the town of Chester was preparing for its bicentennial year (Starbuck 2000).

I was asked by members of the Town of Chester Historical Society if I would help them celebrate in the summer of 1999 by selecting an archeological site that could be dug by local volunteers. Any historical site would be fine, as long as it helped the residents of Chester, and visitors, become more aware of local Adirondack history. Therein lay a problem, because I wasn't sure that anything really important had ever occurred in Chester. Where would I find a site that embodied the virtues of small-town life, or where a famous person had lived, or where the artifacts would reveal the secret vices of a proud old family? Yet if we failed, I could almost see the headline: "Chester Has No History." And so the Chester Historical Society and I embarked on a search for a historic house, a backyard, or a neighborhood where we might dig up insights into the history of one of the Adirondacks' older towns.

The town of Chester was formed from part of the town of Thurman in 1799, but there were dozens of families living there in the ten years preceding. The Meads, Starbucks, Leggetts, and others established farms in the 1790s; two log taverns were built there in the early 1800s at what became known as Chester Four Corners; and local entrepreneurs launched into businesses that included tanning, sheep raising, carding, and lumbering. Most of the first settlers who founded Chester were Quakers, some of whom (the Leggetts and Starbucks) had previously owned sections of the Saratoga battlefield in Stillwater. With the arrival of peace, Quaker homesteaders and military veterans moved north up the Hudson Valley into the southern Adirondacks as land became available.

The Leggetts established a Quaker meetinghouse and cemetery on either side of Tannery Road at the southern end of the village of Chestertown, but they were soon accompanied by plenty of other churches: Baptist (founded ca. 1819), Methodist (ca. 1830), Presbyterian (1833), Roman Catholic (1867), and Episcopal (1884). Land speculators bought and sold lots in the center of the village throughout the nineteenth century, and a total of seventeen small schoolhouses operated in various parts of the town in 1845. Charles Faxon constructed a tannery, which used hemlock bark, in 1849, and he became the wealthiest businessman and landowner in Chestertown. While his second house still stands today as the Upstate Agency Insurance building, his industrial buildings have long been abandoned and decaying. On the north side of Chestertown, housing was created for Faxon's Irish immigrant tannery workers in a neighborhood that was nicknamed "Dublin," and the crossroads of two major highways, Routes 8 and 9, attracted businesses and visitors to what became an amazingly prosperous community. Late nineteenth-century photographs of the center of Chestertown reveal houses ringed by barns, carriage houses, privy houses, sheds, and smokehouses, a far denser cluster of buildings than exists today. Stately elm trees, large grassy lawns, and grand Victorian houses gave an air of prosperity that has not been equaled in the twentieth or twenty-first centuries.

To meet the needs of the growing numbers of tourists visiting the Adirondacks, the lovely Chester House was built in the center of the village in the

6.5.
A postcard view of
the Chester House.

mid-1800s and later acquired by Harry and Althea Downs in the 1880s (fig.
6.5). The Chester House, the last vestige of the glory days of Chestertown, was
a first-class summer resort hotel until tourism waned and decline set in, and
it was finally torn down and burned in 1955. Guests had included the boxer
John L. Sullivan and President James E. Garfield, and I can still remember
watching from the window of my grandmother's apartment over the Chester-
Schroon-Horicon Bank as the wrecking ball struck the tired old building. To
a child of five, it was traumatic to see such an immense structure torn down,
with nothing grand to take its place. Today there is a convenience store and
filling station in that location.

Since then, and especially with the opening of the Adirondack Northway
(Interstate 87) between 1957 and 1967, many of the older businesses have
closed in Chestertown, marking the transition to a community of commuters,
retirees, and young families devoted to raising their children in a safe, idyllic
environment. Chestertown, and indeed the rest of the Adirondacks, have not
become "the land that time forgot," but have learned to proceed cautiously
into the future.

When we started our search for an exciting historic site to dig in Chester,
our only requirement was that it be in the center of the villages of either Chestertown or Pottersville, where passers-by could stop and chat and see our discoveries each weekend. This eliminated from consideration any outlying properties, such as the Leggett and Starbuck homesteads, that still look much the
way they did two centuries ago. A dig around the edges of the Leggett house
would have been especially tempting, because this was a well-documented way

6.6.
The front yard of the Chester Inn in Chestertown, a prominent B&B that welcomed archeology in 1999.

station on the Underground Railroad. Could we find evidence for runaway slaves who were sheltered by a Quaker family as they traveled north through the Adirondacks to Canada (Godine 1998)? It was also impossible to expose any of the house remains in the Dublin community, where the house sites had been destroyed by an expansion of Route 8 in the 1960s. We gave some consideration to the yards around the 1913 Chester Town Hall, which had formerly been a schoolhouse, but the most exciting artifacts probably would have been school supplies lost by my father and his fellow students in the 1920s. Unfortunately, the most altered part of Chestertown appeared to be the very core of the village, where blacktop and parking areas, the epitome of "car culture," now cover what once were green spaces.

But then it hit us. Chestertown does have one property in the center of the village that clearly reveals the way Adirondack life and homes used to be: the home of Harry and Althea Downs that now survives as the Chester Inn (not to be confused with the Chester House), located at 6347 Main Street (Route 9), and still flanked (in the rear) by three sizable barns, carriage stalls, and the most exquisite smokehouse in the Adirondacks (fig. 6.6). There even is an original privy house still attached to the back side of the inn itself. The main house was built by Charles Fowler, a wealthy businessman, between 1830 and 1837 and was purchased by the Downs family in the 1880s. When Harry died in 1950, he left his considerable estate to Fern Clipperd, his slightly eccentric housekeeper and the head waitress at the Chester House. Fern did not alter a thing, and for years she lived alone in the house, rarely using electricity, driving a 1934 Ford up until the 1960s, and chasing away the children who came to sled in the field behind her barns. Thanks to Fern, it was still possible for us to walk into the middle of a well-to-do nineteenth-century estate just a stone's throw from the village center, a crossroads now occupied by the Chester-Schroon-Horicon office of the Glens Falls National Bank, the attractive Panther Mountain Inn, a gas station and "mini mart," and the bank parking lot.

Best of all, Fern's estate had been sold at auction to Bruce and Suzanne Robbins in 1987, and they had beautifully converted the property into a bed and breakfast, the Chester Inn (fig. 6.7). Bruce and Suzanne proposed that we dig in their yards, around the barns, inside the privy house and smokehouse, and any other place where there might be dumps. The picturesque Chester Inn, with all its outbuildings, clearly had more potential to reveal what Chestertown used to look like, a century ago and more, than anything else that remains in the village. We had found our site, and I was about to discover whether the grounds of a B&B in a small Adirondack town had artifacts and a story to tell that could put it on the same map as Maya temples, Egyptian tombs, and all the other great archeological sites of antiquity. The Adirondacks have many hundreds of B&Bs that offer hospitality to travelers from all over the world, but we were now about to generate some new stories to tell to visitors.

Just about every old house or barn has shallow dumps behind its rear doors, as well as a thin scatter of artifacts just about everywhere, which is what historical archeologists term "sheet refuse." The Chester Inn was no exception, and in the rear yard next to the privy house, our team members from the Town of Chester Historical Society found a complete tobacco pipe bowl, lots of pottery sherds of white earthenware, yellowware, and unrefined stoneware, hundreds of butchered animal bones, clam shells, cut and wire nails, fragments of chimneys from kerosene lamps, and bits of window glass. In the same spot, we made a much more interesting discovery, which was the 1898 identification plate from a bicycle, "The D&H," sold by "BUDD BROS MFG," which used to be located at 90 Glen Street in Glens Falls (fig. 6.8).

At one end of the carriage stalls, right on the property line, we dug underneath the crushed rock that marked a former driveway and found whiskey and beer bottles, an apothecary bottle with its glass stopper, a ceramic doorknob, a complete enamelware pot, and two bottles of an early soft drink, bottled by "McCarthy Bros & Martin" in Riverside, New York (just ten miles away). Next to the central barn we discovered hundreds of sherds of pottery and glass, and as families came to visit our dig, their children helped us pick out the sherds of nineteenth-century transfer-printed white earthenware, pieces of pressed glass, and butchered bones. The dump artifacts spanned the entire history

6.7. ▶
Chester House and Chester Inn artifacts being displayed by Bruce Robbins.

6.8. ▶▶
A bicycle identification plate excavated from a test pit behind the Chester Inn.

of Chestertown, from late eighteenth-century tobacco pipes, through black, manganese-glazed redwares from the 1840s, late nineteenth-century sherds from stoneware crocks, jugs, and chamber pots, and recent, twentieth-century bottle caps. We even unearthed a nearly complete sheep or goat skull.

George Wertime, at that time the president of the Town of Chester Historical Society, dug just one pit next to the southernmost barn and was rewarded with a pig skull, fragmented into scores of pieces and lying only a few inches below the ground surface (fig. 6.9). Chances are this came from a pig that had hung in the nearby smokehouse. Few smokehouses have ever been excavated by archeologists, and we of course didn't know what types of artifacts might be inside. The smokehouse that lies about forty-five feet behind the Chester Inn is lined with bricks that are now starting to crumble. It measures just seven by ten feet, and dozens of meat hooks still hang from the ceiling (fig. 6.10). This dark chamber was large enough for only one worker, so Sarah Waite, one of our more experienced diggers, ventured inside each weekend, carrying the buckets of dirt outside to sift on the open lawn (fig. 6.11). She found about four inches of ash, charcoal, and burned bone lying on the floor, with a few meat hooks mixed in, plus small pieces of glass and pottery, and nails.

Best of all, our dig was attracting scores of visitors every weekend, all eager to reminisce about the Chester House, Harry Downs, and Fern Clipperd. It

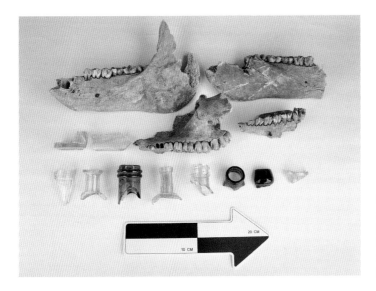

6.9.
Artifacts found behind the Chester Inn. Fragments of a pig's skull appear in the top two rows, and fragments of medicine bottles in the lower rows. One bottle is marked with "J. WHITE."

6.10.
Sarah Waite digging inside the smokehouse behind the Chester Inn in 1999.

6.11.
Sarah Waite sifting dirt outside the smokehouse.

really was a great way to get the "old-timers" of the area to tell their favorite stories, and community involvement became much more important to us than just finding old fragments of history. Most of our visitors were the very young and the very old, and our most dependable digger — Linda Culver — also became the most adept at giving guided tours to everyone, explaining why the home of Charles Fowler and Harry Downs represented the best of Chester's past and how archeology was being used to bring its stories back to life. One of our visitors was Millie Frazier, niece of Fern Clipperd, and she cheerily informed us, "If you dig up any gold coins, half of them are mine!" Even the noted artist Forrest Jones of Pottersville helped out by painting a sign for the front lawn of the Chester Inn, welcoming passers-by to stop and visit the dig (fig. 6.5).

The Excavation of a Privy

As our excavations proceeded, we were gradually preparing ourselves to tackle what would become our most significant site: the privy house. We had already dug two pits just outside the privy, and they had been extremely rich in bottle fragments, some of which were embossed with the word "HAIR." Few young people today can appreciate how important, and ubiquitous, outhouses were in the days before running water, but every home had them, and most privies became repositories for trash once they ceased to be used for human waste. Historical archeologists (and bottle collectors) dearly love these structures, and often the most improper, secret, and surprising of artifacts are hidden inside privies, largely undisturbed by subsequent generations. Not everyone likes the notion of digging a privy, but the truth is that the feces inside have often been removed or decomposed, so the task of excavating a privy is not always that unpleasant for the archeologist. The literature describing these structures is extensive and often quite entertaining (Barlow 1992; Kilroy 1996; Gruse 2014).

The privy at the Chester Inn had been a three-holer, measuring six by six feet. There was a smaller child's hole in the center, so the hole diameters measured 10 ½ inches, 8 inches, and 10 ½ inches. The upper part of the outhouse is now used as a storage closet, so we couldn't descend into it from above. Instead, we went in from the back, where the hinged door (to remove excrement) had once been (fig. 6.12). The first to crawl inside was Cheryl Walker, who had arrived to write a newspaper story and stayed to dig with us. Cheryl spent a Sunday afternoon excitedly uncovering hundreds of crumpled fragments of newspaper, many covered with rather suspicious-looking brown stains (figs. 6.13 and 6.14). These pages were from the *Daily Mirror*, the *World*, the *Evening Star*, and the *Troy Record*, spanning the 1910s and 1920s. The newspapers had usually sold for one penny each. Articles had catchy titles such as "Secret Bride

6.12. ▲▲
Cheryl Walker crawling out from underneath the privy house.

6.13. ▲
George Wertime holding pieces of newspaper found inside the privy. Fortunately he was not bothered at all by the brown stains.

6.14. ◄
Well-used newspapers found inside the privy.

of Boy Husband" and "Burglars' Banquet" (*Daily Mirror*, Oct. 27, 1920), reminding us how little tabloid stories have changed over the years. We were, of course, disappointed to find no "brown" pages from Sears, Roebuck catalogs.

I could easily relate to this backyard feature at the Chester Inn because I too had grown up with a three-holer, and whenever the springs that supplied our farmhouse with water went dry (several times each year), which meant no working flush toilet, we would trudge out to the privy that was attached to the side of our woodshed. Privies continued to be used long after indoor plumbing became standard in most houses, and typically new holes were dug nearby whenever a privy hole became really filthy; the homeowner would then fill in the old hole with trash. A backyard could easily have several filled-in privy holes, wonderful sites for the archeologist.

A week after we started, Cheryl was not able to join us, and I became the volunteer inside the privy house. It was a fascinating introduction to nineteenth- and twentieth-century America when I spent a day exposing whiskey bottles, a cork labeled "GILBEY'S" (gin), druggist bottles, part of a douche bag, pieces of a kerosene lamp shade, salve jars of milk glass, shell-edged pearlware, white earthenware, a shattered manganese-glazed redware teapot with flower decoration, a bottle of hair cream (labeled "LYON'S KATHAIRON   NEW YORK   FOR THE HAIR"), tobacco pipe stems, chicken bones, a cow's rib, peach pits, a clothespin, literally hundreds of cut nails, and even a peanut shell (figs. 6.15 and 6.16). One possible interpretation for this assemblage is that Harry and Althea Downs had not wanted to carry garbage outdoors in the winter and instead pitched everything into the privy.

Facing page

6.15. ▲
Artifacts found on the surface of the privy, including peach pits, a clothespin, tops and bottoms from jars of milk glass, a broken cup of whiteware, the rim from a large whiteware platter with shell-edged decoration, the tin top from a container of talcum powder, and a round, amber-colored bottle that is embossed on the bottom with "P.D. & Co. 11 12." The milk glass was labeled "DR. J. PARKER PRAY ESTABLISHED 1868 NEW YORK." (These contained toilet preparations for removing stains from the skin and fingernails and for bleaching and manicuring the nails.)

6.16. ▼
Artifacts found inside the privy, including four fragments of tobacco pipes, a very rusted razor blade, the rusted buckle from an undergarment, a lid and sherds from a black-glazed red earthenware bowl, a sherd of gray, unrefined stoneware, three fragments of a clear glass bottle that reads "& Moore Co.   Adelphia," four fragments of a clear glass bottle that reads "LYON'S" on one side, "KATHAIRON" on another side, "YORK" on a third side, and "FOR THE" on the fourth side.

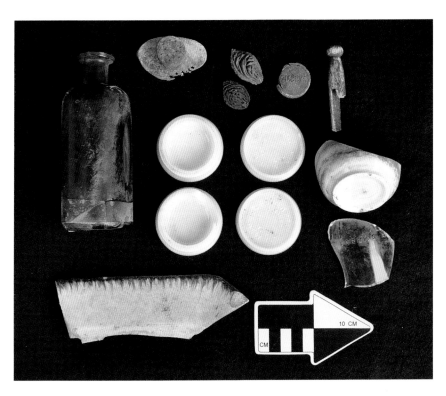

Lyon's "Kathairon for the Hair" was a nineteenth-century hair and scalp treatment made by the Lyon Manufacturing Company in Brooklyn, New York; it was purported to be a cure for baldness and gray hair. Other bottles found inside the privy with diagnostic lettering included two tops and two bases of milk glass jars (2 1/8 inches in diameter) that read "DR. J. PARKER PRAY   ESTAB-LISHED 1868   NEW YORK." These represented toilet preparations for removing stains from the skin and fingernails and for bleaching and manicuring the nails. We also found a round, amber-colored bottle with embossing on the bottom that read "P.D. & Co. 11 12." We even found much of the rim from a large white earthenware platter with shell-edged decoration, and the tin top from a container of talcum powder.

There is probably no tasteful way to describe what it is like to excavate inside an old, dusty privy house, but for the dozens of visitors who watched as buckets of dirt were pushed out through the back, clean-out panel, it was a chance for ribald bathroom humor. After all, the hometown son who had gone away to earn a PhD in archeology had now been reduced to cleaning out an outhouse. Inside the privy house it was hot, there were cobwebs everywhere, my lungs were filling with fine powder — probably a mix of lime and decomposed excrement — and every so often a confused chipmunk darted inside, saw me, and dashed out again. The first two to four inches underneath the privy holes contained the most newspaper fragments, while the next four to five inches were moist, dank earth, underlain by sterile, yellowish-brown sand. It didn't really smell, but after removing thirty-six cubic feet of privy soil, my lungs were congested with powdered feces, and my throat was raw for days afterward. I had tried to wear a respirator mask as a precaution, but the mask had fogged my eyeglasses so much that I gave up, and the result was to fill my lungs with filth. Still, while it wasn't exactly another King Tut's tomb, it was an amazing cross-section of the ordinary, the profane, and the little things that a Chestertown family had wanted to hide from sight. The many bits of newspaper were certainly the best part because, brown stains and all, they had been preserved beautifully in this cavelike environment.

Final Thoughts

After listening to the comments of hundreds of visitors, and examining the thousands of artifacts that came from this backyard in Chestertown, I am pleased to say that archeology became a novel and productive way for one Adirondack community to celebrate its bicentennial. The artifacts by themselves were mostly commonplace, but they show how Chestertown, and the surrounding region, was increasingly becoming part of a world economy, with residents making purchases over an ever-larger area. I have nothing against the parades, exhibits, or pamphlets that mark most bicentennials, but the purpose of a town bicentennial is to commemorate two hundred years of history. The small bits of history that came from the ground at the Chester Inn provided a lot of visitors with tangible clues to the past, a time when there was a great resort hotel practically across the street, before the era of the smaller B&Bs that now blanket every town in the Adirondacks. Yet Chestertown's archeological dig also tells us that it once was acceptable to throw trash behind your house; that families smoked their own meat; that you could throw "contraband" into the family privy; and that those who imbibed sometimes hid liquor bottles in the yard. The "BUDD BROS" bicycle identification plate also reminds us that many of the changes that occurred in small Adirondack towns came about because of the improvement of the roads, which brought increased mobility and greater prosperity to the region. Bicycle trails are everywhere today, and bicycle tourism is one of the best clean, green incentives bringing fresh visitors to the Adirondacks ("Bike Tourism Should Pedal Forward," 2017).

We cannot rebuild the grand hotels like the Chester House, and the stately elm trees are gone forever, but archeology can keep reminding us of those times, and well-preserved properties like the Chester Inn can help promote local preservation efforts. Every Adirondack community needs to preserve its green spaces, its older houses, the outbuildings around them, and the accompanying archeological sites. With careful management of these resources, Adirondack towns will still be great places to live for at least the next two hundred years.

7.1.
Chester Rural Cemetery.

LIFE AND DEATH IN THE ADIRONDACKS

The Adirondack Park contains literally hundreds of community graveyards (figs. 7.1 and 7.2), as well as innumerable small, family burial plots. In addition, there are a great many unmarked graves of Native Americans and of soldiers who died during the early military campaigns in the region. The grounds of Fort Ticonderoga, in particular, contain the carefully protected remains of French, British, and American soldiers who died there throughout the eighteenth century, typically resting in unmarked graves.

Yet while an individual community may have dozens of graveyards, very little forensic anthropology or forensic archeology has ever been conducted in the Adirondacks. The most notable exception to this is at Fort William Henry on Lake George, where some fascinating work has been done with the burials of soldiers from the French and Indian War (figs. 7.3 and 7.4). This work has been extensively published elsewhere (e.g., Baker and Rieth 2000; Starbuck 2014, chap. 6; Blackwell 1996), so it does not need detailed coverage here. All the same, the remains of early soldiers are able to provide an amazing amount of information about disease, trauma, diet, and the overall demographics of the first Europeans who arrived in the southern Adirondacks.

However, just outside the Adirondack Park, an excellent forensics project was conducted in the summer and fall of 1997 at an eighteenth-century Quaker burying ground at the corner of Bay and Quaker Roads in the town of Queensbury (fig. 7.5). This crucial "rescue" effort, directed in the field by Sarah Majot, then of Collamer & Associates, recorded a 1765–1837 cemetery, the very earliest in Queensbury (Collamer & Associates 2003). The cemetery was about to be dug up to create a small shopping mall, and an archeological survey was needed, because Quaker custom at that time did not allow for the use of gravestones. The Quaker Burying Ground (the "Queensbury Friends Cemetery") had long been forgotten, and even property deeds did not mention the burial site. After a loud, public outcry by those who did not want the dead to be disturbed, archeologists found six burials that had been bisected by the foundation of a preexisting building, and some burials had had posts driven through them. Twenty-four burials were identified altogether, out of about eighty burials that are known to have been in the cemetery. Four human burials had to be moved, along with three animal burials. After many months

PINE SLAB

7.2. ▲▲
Union Cemetery in North Creek.

7.3. ◀
One of the soldiers' skeletons in the cemetery at Fort William Henry, prior to its removal from display in 1993.

7.4. ▲
Maria Liston and Brenda Baker (*at rear*) with their students, examining soldiers' skeletons from the cemetery at Fort William Henry.

7.5.
Site of the Quaker Burying
Ground in Queensbury.

of fieldwork and analysis, the outcome of this project was that intensive, modern archeology helped to save the remains of some of Queensbury's earliest citizens.

The Death and Rebirth of Jane McCrea through Modern Science

A second project on the edge of the Adirondack Park lies just a few miles farther south. In the Hudson River town of Fort Edward lie the remains of one of the most tragic yet fascinating heroines in the early history of the United States, and it is only through the latest forensic analysis that her story may now be told in detail. Few accounts from the eighteenth century are as poignant as that of Jane McCrea, a Scottish-Presbyterian woman who was murdered and scalped in 1777 while en route to marry her Tory fiancé, David Jones (fig. 7.6).

It is hard to resist the image of a lovely damsel in distress, and Jane's sad end in Fort Edward prompted thousands of Americans to oppose the British Crown and to fight against the army of General John Burgoyne at the battle

7.6.
The grave of Jane
McCrea inside its
enclosure in Union
Cemetery in Fort
Edward. This 2004
limestone monu-
ment has replaced
an earlier 1852
gravestone.

of Saratoga. The brutality of her death at the hands of Native American warriors who accompanied Burgoyne was skillfully exploited by Patriot leaders as
they sought recruits, and so her youthful demise at the age of twenty-three or
twenty-four became one of the defining moments of the American Revolution.
Americans did not want their wives and daughters to become casualties in the
struggle for independence (Namias 1993; Wilson 1853).

While Jane's life appears to have been rather uneventful, the horrific cir-
cumstances of her death elevated her to the status of an American icon, one
of the few women of that time widely remembered for falling victim to British oppression. Jane's memory was subsequently kept alive through the many
etchings and watercolors that depicted her tragic death. From John Vanderlyn's
magnificent 1804 painting, *The Death of Jane McCrea*, now in the Wadsworth
Atheneum Museum of Art in Hartford, Connecticut (fig. 7.7), to F. C. Yohn's
1912 image prepared for the Glens Falls Insurance Company, Jane was invariably portrayed as the flower of lovely young womanhood. Artists sometimes
painted her seated upon a horse beneath the tree where her body was later
found, and she always appeared surrounded by the warriors who were about
to take her scalp and her life. Burgoyne's use of Indian allies clearly helped to
turn the colonial population against British authority, and some of the earlier
artistic images of Jane McCrea's death portrayed the Native Americans with
the faces of demons, reflecting the intense hatred of native peoples that sometimes lingered after the colonial wars.

7.7.
The Murder of Jane McCrea, 1804. John Vanderlyn, American, 1775–1852. Oil on canvas, 32½ x 26½ in. (82.6 × 67.4 cm). Courtesy of Allen Phillips / Wadsworth Atheneum Museum of Art, Hartford, CT. Purchased by subscription, 1855.4.

The Jane McCrea story certainly evokes grim thoughts, but Jane continues to be celebrated throughout northern New York State, and especially in Fort Edward, the community where she spent her final days in July of 1777. While all other residents of that town had fled from Burgoyne's approaching army, only Jane and a young man, Norman Morrison, stayed behind in the house of Sarah McNeil, the grandmother of her good friend Polly Hunter. History recounts that a band of Native Americans dispatched from Burgoyne's army dragged Jane, Sarah, and Norman from their hiding place in the cellar of that house, and they were escorted in the direction of the British camp. Jane was mounted on a horse, but the elderly Sarah McNeil was reportedly too corpulent to ride astride a horse and was forced to walk. Somewhere in the vicinity of the present-day Fort Edward School, Jane was killed, either by Indians quarreling over the reward they hoped to receive for escorting her to David Jones, or by a musket ball fired from Patriot forces in the distance. In contrast, Sarah survived the war and lived for another twenty-two years in Fort Edward. When Sarah died in 1799 at the age of seventy-seven, she left behind a considerable estate, and she was buried in a brick vault in the town's State Street Cemetery.

For modern-day residents of Fort Edward, the death of Jane McCrea is seen as the most important event in their town's history. The oft-repeated story of Jane and Sarah is not to be tampered with, even though many questions remain about Jane's age, appearance, and cause of death. Jane's hair, in particular, has been the subject of endless speculation, given its status as arguably the most famous scalp in American history. We know that David Jones identified Jane's hair in the midst of a pile of scalps that Indians had turned in for bounties at the British camp, but was it raven (black), as is often suggested, or was she a brunette or blond, as depicted in much later paintings? Jane's remains achieved celebrity status, but confusion also lingered because of the periodic exhumation of her body or skeleton.

Jane had originally been buried three miles south of Fort Edward in 1777; but she was later exhumed and moved to State Street Cemetery in 1822, where she was placed next to or on top of Sarah McNeil's remains; and then on to Union Cemetery in 1852. Both cemeteries were easily accessible to visitors, and the desire to view the grave of such a famous woman was certainly understandable. However, no one knew whether Jane's remains were actually in her marked grave, or whether nineteenth-century souvenir hunters had removed most of her bones. This was a very real possibility, because historical accounts from 1852 claimed that "the leading citizens" of Fort Edward had stolen some of her bones at the time of the last exhumation, including her skull, ribs, and "tibial bones" (Hill 1928). All the same, for many years tour buses have made a point of stopping at Union Cemetery to view the limestone monument atop Jane's third and final grave and to decry the fate of this unfortunate woman.

The Forensic Analysis of Jane McCrea

Many residents of Fort Edward would have been content to keep telling the Jane McCrea story in its traditional form, relying solely on paintings and local folklore to keep Jane's memory alive. However, this did not allow for the diligence of Jane's oldest living relative, Mrs. Mary McCrea Deeter, of Wichita, Kansas. For many years Deeter faithfully wrote to Fort Edward's town historian, Paul McCarty, decrying Jane's gradual slide into oblivion. Jane McCrea was no longer nationally known as the martyr who inspired the victory at Saratoga and instead was remembered only by a handful of New Yorkers and specialists on the American Revolution. Deeter wanted Jane to return to her once-prominent position in American history and wondered if anything could be done locally. Somewhat impulsively, I wrote to her in May of 2002 and asked if she would agree to a forensic investigation that would reopen Jane's grave, establish through mitochondrial DNA (mtDNA) testing whether it was Jane in the grave, and begin the process of seeking the return of any missing bones.

Mrs. Deeter was 97 at the time (and has subsequently passed away, at the age of 104), but she readily gave her consent and offered locks of her own hair and her grandson Ben Williams's hair for mtDNA testing. And most touchingly, she offered the hair of "my daughter Diana Williams when not looking, as she is against this examination." I could not help but be charmed at her clever ingenuity — Mrs. Deeter was not going to be stopped when it came to learning more about her famous relative. At this point I engaged an attorney, William L. Nikas of Hudson Falls, whose office prepared the petition to the Supreme Court of Washington County that Deeter later signed.

In assembling the forensic investigative team, I first called Dr. Lowell J. Levine, a world-renowned forensic odontologist who is codirector of the Medicolegal Investigations Unit, New York State Police, and he in turn contacted Colonel Brion Smith, chief deputy medical examiner and director, Department of Defense DNA Registry. Brion agreed to conduct the mtDNA testing at government expense. Next, we contacted Dr. Anthony Falsetti, then at the University of Florida in Gainesville, who was director of the C. A. Pound Human Identification Laboratory and a noted forensic anthropologist, and Herbert W. Buckley, director of forensic imaging, New York State Police, and one of the leading facial reconstruction experts in the world. For the genealogical and historical research necessary to prepare the court petition, we consulted with Eileen Hannay, at that time the manager of the Rogers Island Visitors Center; she had studied Jane McCrea's history for the previous twelve years. The actual digging of the grave site would be conducted by members of the Adirondack Chapter of the New York State Archaeological Association. As with any contemporary murder investigation, the team needed to be large, specialized, and above all secretive, because we did not want anything to happen that might mar the family's desire for respect and scientific accuracy.

csi Fort Edward

What followed was a phenomenon that Dr. Levine dubbed "csi Fort Edward." What I had not anticipated was that once Mrs. Deeter's petition was approved by the court, a veritable flood of letters to the editor, editorials, petitions, and political cartoons chastised me and my team for being ghoulish and disrespectful, and the mayor at that time claimed that the village of Fort Edward would "lose its history" if we were allowed to proceed. Still, we were already beginning to satisfy Deeter's wishes, because we had motivated a host of individuals, who had never before shown the slightest interest in Jane McCrea, to passionately call for our heads!

With expert assistance from the M. B. Kilmer Funeral Home in Fort Edward, a team of nearly two dozen archeologists and forensic scientists opened the grave on April 9, 2003, with Deeter's grandson Ben Williams in attendance to ensure that her wishes would be observed. Beginning at six-thirty in the morning, Ward Memorials of South Glens Falls lifted the monument off the grave, and the Fort Miller Group installed a court-ordered tent around the gravesite so that only family members and scientists would be able to see the human remains. We then began to dig through the soft yellow sand that had not been disturbed since 1852. It was about noon when we discovered the remains of two women, one young and one very old, with their bones thoroughly intermingled inside a dark stain (fig. 7.8) — all that remained of a wood box that had once measured 20 by 24 inches, by 8–9 inches deep. Only one skull was present in the grave (fig. 7.9), and it belonged to the older woman, toothless, big-boned, and between 5 feet 6 inches and 5 feet 10 in height. We assumed the younger woman to be a rather petite Jane McCrea (between 5 feet and 5 feet 4 inches), but the identity of the older woman was definitely a mystery. History had left no record of anyone buried together with Jane in 1852.

A few irate protesters attempted to interfere with the exhumation and were quickly chased away by the police. That evening, just before the grave was filled in, a reburial service was conducted over the remains by Rev. John Barclay of the First Presbyterian Church in Glens Falls. When the grave was sealed, with the bones inside a new, plain pine box, we assumed that this would be the last time that anyone would look upon the bones of Jane McCrea and her mysterious companion.

Before the refilling of the grave, Anthony Falsetti had removed four small bone samples for mtDNA testing, and they became part of the "chain of custody," not to be tampered with before the analyses were completed. On the next day these were sent off to the Armed Forces Institute of Pathology in Washington, D.C., which had agreed to reconstruct profiles of the "ancient DNA" from anyone we found in the grave. Fortunately, in the year that followed, DNA analyst Carna Meyer in the Armed Forces DNA Identification Laboratory was able to gradually amplify and identify the mtDNA profiles from the four bone samples, and at that time they were the oldest war-related samples yet tested by that laboratory.

Two Women in the Grave

Acting on a hunch that Jane McCrea's bones might still have been lying with those of Sarah McNeil, we obtained modern mtDNA samples from Mary Brown, a seventh-generation maternal descendant of Sarah McNeil who lived in Queensbury. When two of our "ancient DNA" samples matched Mary Brown's modern mtDNA, we knew that the older skeleton in the grave was that of Sarah McNeil, long thought to still rest in the State Street Cemetery. History

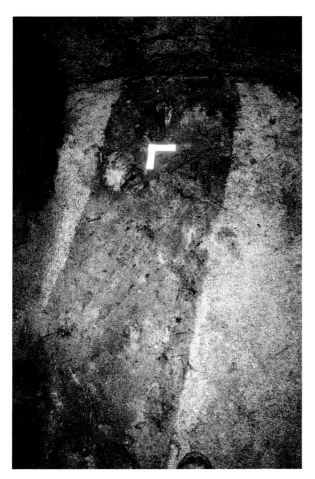

7.8. ◀
The dark stain of Jane McCrea's burial trench as exposed on April 9, 2003. A skull is visible at the top left.

7.9. ▼
The skull found in the grave, later determined to be that of Sarah McNeil. Note the missing teeth and bone regrowth (over the root sockets), indicating an elderly individual far too old to be Jane McCrea.

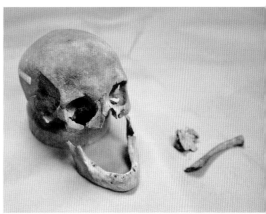

had left no record that Sarah's bones had been moved along with Jane's bones to Union Cemetery in 1852, where both ended up together within the same grave and the same wood box.

This was perhaps the most wonderful finding in all our research, but it also introduced a new element: we now had to seek permissions from the relatives and descendants of Sarah McNeil, as well as the relatives of Jane McCrea, if we wanted to conduct any additional work. Still, both families had an equal stake in what happened next, and it was agreed that the commingled skeletons needed to be separated. Each woman deserved her own coffin and her own grave. Attorney Nikas drafted a second petition to the Supreme Court of Washington County, this time to be signed by Mary Brown and with a supporting letter from Mary McCrea Deeter.

On receipt of a second court order, we returned to the grave on April 22, 2005, reopened the coffin we had placed there in 2003, and conducted a far

7.10.
Sarah van Ryckevorsel (*foreground*)
and Linda White reopening the grave
and the plain pine box in 2005.

more thorough investigation than had been possible before. This time it was women who were at the center of the investigation in every possible way, as two women signed the petition that went to the court, two women archeologists did the actual digging (fig. 7.10), and it was the skeletons of the two most famous local women of the eighteenth century who were being exhumed.

As Anthony Falsetti methodically separated the bones of the two skeletons, he was able to discern that the skeleton of Jane McCrea was in a comparable state to that of Sarah McNeil. In fact, even though Sarah's skull was present, some of her limb bones were missing, revealing that when bones were stolen from the grave in 1852, more bones had been taken from Sarah's skeleton than from Jane's. As the two skeletons lay side by side on the laboratory tables in the Rogers Island Visitors Center in Fort Edward, it was clear that we never would have known how complete Jane McCrea's skeleton is today if we had not gone into the grave for the second time (fig. 7.11). All Jane's limb bones survive inside the grave, even though both women lack most of their ribs, vertebrae, hand, and foot bones. These are the more spongy "cancellous" bones that tend

7.11.
The skeletal remains of Sarah McNeil (*left*, with skull) and Jane McCrea (*right*) laid out on the laboratory tables of the Rogers Island Visitors Center in Fort Edward.

to deteriorate more rapidly in acidic soil. There were no signs of trauma on any of the bones of the smaller woman's skeleton, so we will probably never know the cause of death for Jane McCrea. Also, with Jane's skull missing, we will never be able to gaze upon or reconstruct her face.

Sarah McNeil provided us with a much better opportunity for facial reconstruction, and digital photos of Sarah's seventy-seven-year-old skull were transmitted to Herbert Buckley, who reconstructed her face within a single day (figs. 7.12, 7.13, and 7.14). We were thus able to show Sarah's features to two of her descendants — John and Fred Austin — just before Sarah's and Jane's bones were placed inside new coffins and buried in adjacent graves on April 23, 2005. This time our second burial service was led by Rev. Jason Santalucia of the First Presbyterian Church of Hudson Falls, and in this service it was possible to acknowledge the identities of both women, thanks to the mtDNA testing.

Making This Story Relevant to Modern Audiences

The forensic investigation had a fascinating "ripple effect" throughout the community, and town historian Paul McCarty and the Fort Edward Historical Association were able to purchase and place a new limestone monument atop Jane McCrea's grave in 2004 (fig. 7.6), followed by a second monument on top of Sarah McNeil's grave on Memorial Day in 2006. In August 2004, reenactors in Fort Edward were able to re-create on camera the events leading up to Jane's death (figs. 7.15 and 7.16), and in November 2004, the History Channel aired the program "Buried Secrets of the Revolutionary War," featuring the history and forensic investigation of Jane McCrea and Sarah McNeil. A very old story

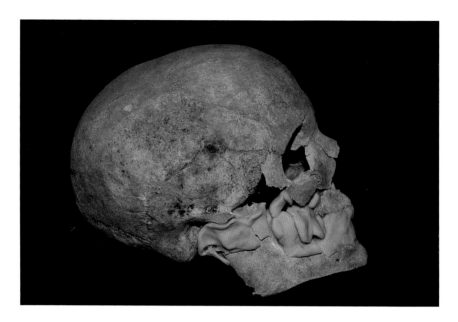

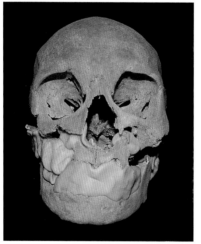

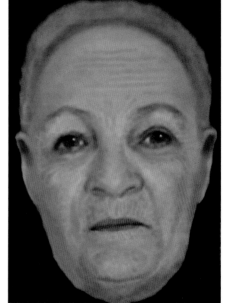

7.12. ▲▲
A side view of the skull of Sarah McNeil. The clay
has been added to permit scanning, necessary if
the face is to be reconstructed.

7.13. ▲
A frontal view of the "face" of Sarah McNeil.

7.14. ▶
The fully reconstructed face of Sarah McNeil,
re-created by Herbert Buckley, director, Forensic
Imaging, New York State Police.

7.15. ◀◀
The modern-day woman, Sarah van Ryckevorsel, selected to portray Jane McCrea on the History Channel. Here her hair (a wig) is being adjusted just prior to her being scalped.

7.16. ◀
The reenactment of the scalping of Jane McCrea in August 2004 for the History Channel.

of a murder that may have changed the course of the American Revolution had become relevant once again.

While aspects of this research were stressful and time-consuming, it was comforting to know that we played a role in helping Mary McCrea Deeter to realize a lifelong dream. Both local and national media gave extensive coverage to the story, even though there was intensive debate about whether it was appropriate to dig up a figure as beloved as Jane McCrea. However, very few good women's stories survive from the frontier of eighteenth-century America, and unquestionably both Jane and Sarah represent women who were strong and self-reliant as they bravely waited for the approaching British army in 1777. While they clearly met with misfortune, their stirring story became a catalyst that helped lead to the American victory at Saratoga, and so their role must not be forgotten. Artifacts pertaining to Jane and Sarah have long been on display in the Fort House Museum in Fort Edward, and a totally new exhibit telling their stories — both historically and forensically — opened in 2015 in the Rogers Island Visitors Center (fig. 7.17). For the people of New York, the story of Jane McCrea has become current and relevant through modern science, and the results of the investigation have been published in detail (Starbuck 2004b, 2006a, 2006b).

7.17.
A very new exhibit of Sarah McNeil (*seated left*) and Jane McCrea (*standing right*) in the Rogers Island Visitors Center. The mirror on the wall (*left*) is from the Revolutionary War period. The digital screens on the railing in the foreground show scenes from the reconstruction of Sarah's face (*left screen*) and from the two exhumations in Union Cemetery (*right screen*).

In hindsight, our forensic work has had an interesting effect on the people of Fort Edward. Some responded with anger and suspicion at the time of the first exhumation, perhaps thinking that outsiders and scientists were seeking celebrity at the expense of their town's beloved heroine. Fortunately, there was a softening of that attitude over time, and the second exhumation was accompanied by none of the controversy of the first. In fact, most seemed very proud that "their" very own Jane McCrea had become a topic of national discussion and debate and that the very latest scientific techniques were used locally to focus on some of the most interesting events of the American Revolution. Jane McCrea and Sarah McNeil had been thrust into the limelight once again, and their stories would have a lasting impact by increasing the attention given to the lives of early women in northern New York State.

8.1.
The "Town Hall cabin" of the most famous Adirondack hermit, Noah John Rondeau, on display at the Adirondack Experience, on Blue Mountain Lake.

WHAT DOES THE FUTURE HOLD?

EIGHT

I am pleased to say that Adirondack archeology has now come full circle. When I grew up in this region, the historical sites that were stressed were the Great Camps and impressive architectural survivals, many of which are still standing today (Kaiser 1982; Gilborn 2000; Tolles 2003). The nonprofit historic preservation organization known as AARCH (Adirondack Architectural Heritage), based in Keeseville, promotes the stewardship of these sites and sponsors outstanding tours to historic locations throughout the Adirondack Park (Longstreth 2017). We have also been fortunate to have great stories to read about everyday life in the Adirondacks, such as *Bears, Bibles, and a Boy*, which Jesse David Roberts wrote in Brant Lake in 1961, just a few miles from my home. Roberts was the third son of an Adirondack bear trapper, and his tales about his father's bear-hunting exploits were especially exciting because they were true!

But now the region that supposedly had no archeological sites has been shown to have numerous Native American camps, huge numbers of industrial ruins, and "lost towns" of every possible type. As American archeologists are increasingly unable to conduct fieldwork at major sites in other countries, and because many of the earliest and best Native American sites have already been dug, sites in the Adirondacks will soon beckon to us more than ever before. Also, the public and private emphasis on keeping the Adirondacks "forever wild" will continue to ensure that few sites will be "built over" or destroyed by new construction. This high rate of retention of historic ruins will no doubt ensure that the Adirondacks will become an ever-more-popular research destination for future archeologists who recognize the many "survivals" in the North Country. Increasingly, this region will provide stimulating topics for the master's theses and doctoral dissertations of the next generation.

In the future we will also enjoy digging up the home sites and dumps of some of the more fascinating rascals or individualists who have lived in the Adirondacks, such as the best-known of the Adirondack hermits, Noah John Rondeau, who lived for long stretches in the Cold River area in the western High Peaks (Wolff 2010). He will forever be known as "the Mayor of Cold River City" (population 1), and his story is told quite charmingly at the Adirondack Experience on Blue Mountain Lake (fig. 8.1). My uncle, Robert Starbuck, who enjoyed hiking the mountains of the Adirondacks (he was one of the "forty-sixers," having climbed the forty-six peaks of the Adirondacks), loved telling about his occasional meetings with Rondeau, and that would make it almost "personal" if it were ever possible for me to conduct archeology at one of his semi-log-cabin sites.

What do I most wish that I could personally explore and then excavate in the Adirondack Mountains? It is probably a tie between brothels and abandoned villages — brothels because the mountains are sometimes presented as so clean and pure that my mischievous side would like to "liven up" that staid image a bit with stories about real people who led checkered lives. On the other hand, we historical archeologists seek to tell rich stories about community life, and abandoned communities in mountainous areas permit us to examine the lifestyles, occupations, and vernacular architecture of those who ultimately left their Adirondack homes and moved on to other parts of the country. To these "lost towns" or "ghost towns" I would also like to add Prohibition sites, privies, and perhaps some of the Great Camps. After all, the artifacts left behind by "ordinary" Adirondackers are probably quite different from those discarded by wealthy visitors to the Great Camps, and most archeologists love the opportunity to compare the material culture of those from radically different strata of society. It is one thing to claim that visitors ate, drank, and dressed far better than "locals" could ever afford to do, but it is infinitely better to explore the dumps of both groups and then to compare what they actually consumed. For example, if piles of wine bottles were found eroding out of an earthen bank at Camp Santanoni near Newcomb, once the summer home of the Robert Pruyn family, an archeologist would first check to see whether these were expensive vintages, and we would then start making comparisons by digging up the dumps of the less affluent, year-round residents in the region.

In preparing this volume, I drove down many back roads, viewed some magnificent natural scenery, and saw an abundance of abandoned cellar holes, decaying houses, ancient farm machinery rusting in the fields, sawmills that have gone out of business, and any number of cemeteries and dump sites. For those who live locally, we take many of these features for granted because they are so common in the Adirondack Mountains. But everything should be thought of as an incipient archeological site, with its story just waiting to be told. Cellar holes, in particular, are ubiquitous across our region, and just a few days ago, I drove past one such feature on Pucker Street in Warrensburg, noticing how the open cellar hole had been recently filled with brush (fig. 8.2) and how apple trees still grew nearby. This is an archeological site, just as surely as an abandoned Native American campsite or a Revolutionary War fort. It's just that we have been spoiled by the old and the exotic, and in time we will come to realize that the near and recent sites of the past century have great value as well because they tell the story of our own immediate ancestors.

For every abandoned cellar hole in the Adirondacks, there must surely be at least one abandoned privy house. Archeologists absolutely love to explore the trash dropped inside old privies once they ceased to be used, and I cannot drive past an abandoned outhouse without wanting to stop, run to the rear clean-out panel, and go exploring inside. I recently experienced that feeling as I drove down Old Mine Road in Hague, looking for the site of the graphite mine, and I hit the brake as I saw a small, red, intact-looking outhouse on the side of the road (fig. 8.3). Are privies a bit gross? Sure! But that is exactly the sort of context where we can discover the things that were deliberately hidden from polite society.

The tasteful, genteel topics are typically described in family diaries and journals, while the not-so-proper things were thrown or fell into the family privy hole. As an extreme example of this, historical archeologists especially like to tell the story of the urban renewal project that took place in the former Tucson, Arizona, red light district around 1970. As many, many privies were explored, there was a fascinating parade of liquor bottles, six-guns, and fetuses to be found inside the privy holes. That is not to say that such things would ever be found in an Adirondack outhouse; but it would still be fun to have a look inside as many privies as possible in order to discover the profane, the

8.2.
An abandoned cellar hole about one hundred feet from the side of Pucker Street in Warrensburg. Apple trees, probably planted when the house was still standing, are just out of the picture.

8.3.
A privy on Old Mine Road in Hague, still in excellent condition in 2017.

8.4.
Elephant Rock in Hague, on the side of Route 8.

contraband, hidden by our ancestors in the one spot where they were sure we would never want to look.

Will anything truly amazing or unique ever be found in the Adirondack Mountains, something that can be ranked among the very best archeological discoveries in the world? That is certainly hard to answer, but every archeologist is inherently a dreamer. Our "best" find will forever be the discovery that we make tomorrow, so we will always be looking for something new and provocative.

Just a few weeks ago, I was driving along Route 8 in the eastern Adirondacks and saw what appeared to be an enormous stone elephant on the side of the highway. For contemporary passers-by, this might appear to be the attraction known among local residents as Elephant Rock, a large rock painted so as to have the appearance of an oversize elephant (fig. 8.4). However, some future archeologist will no doubt argue that this is one of the best twentieth-century artifacts ever created in the Adirondacks, a discovery that will provoke speculation for generations to come. The slightly absurd, the funky or banal creations of our time, may well be regarded by future generations as the greatest discoveries of all. The last frontier of archeology will no doubt be the wonderful sites that are close to home, the creations of our own culture.

APPENDIX

Adirondack Attractions with Collections and Exhibits
of Interest to Archeologists (in alphabetical order)

1. Adirondack Experience (formerly the Adirondack Museum)
   9097 State Route 30, Blue Mountain Lake, NY 12812
   (518) 352-7311
   www.adirondackexperience.com

The Adirondack Experience in the hamlet of Blue Mountain Lake is a museum dedicated to preserving the history of the Adirondacks. Historic structures range from a log hotel to a one-room schoolhouse. The museum offers workshops on such topics as logging, boats, outdoor recreation, mining, craftsmanship, and fine arts.

2. Clinton County Historical Association and Museum
   98 Ohio Road, Plattsburgh, NY 12903
   (518) 561-0340
   www.clintoncountyhistorical.org

The Clinton County Historical Association and Museum maintains a regionally and nationally significant collection of more than thirty thousand objects, including prints, photographs, paintings, folk art, textiles, furniture, musical instruments, letters, diaries, posters, jewelry, agricultural equipment, maps, postcards, ephemera, documents, and rare reference books.

3. Crown Point State Historic Site
   21 Grandview Drive, Crown Point, NY 12928
   (518) 597-4667

Crown Point State Historic Site is the location of the French-built Fort Saint-Frédéric (1734–1759) as well as the British-built fort (commenced in 1759). The ruins of both forts are operated as a historic attraction by the State of New York.

4. Fort Ticonderoga
   102 Fort Ti Road, Ticonderoga, NY
   (518) 585-2821
   www.fortticonderoga.org

Fort Ticonderoga, earlier known as Fort Carillon, is a large eighteenth-century star fort built by the French at a narrows near the south end of Lake Champlain. It was constructed under the supervision of Canadian-born French military engineer Michel Chartier de Lotbinière, Marquis de Lotbinière, between October 1755 and 1757. It was of strategic importance during the eighteenth-century colonial conflicts between Great Britain and France, and again played an important role during the American Revolutionary War.

5. Fort William Henry
   48 Canada Street, Lake George, NY
   (518) 964-6647
   www.fwhmuseum.com

Fort William Henry was a British fort at the southern end of Lake George. It is best known as the site of atrocities committed against the surrendered British and provincial troops following a successful French siege in 1757, an event portrayed in James Fenimore Cooper's novel *The Last of the Mohicans*, first published in 1826. The fort was first excavated and then reconstructed in the 1950s.

6. Goodsell Museum
   2993 State Route 28, Old Forge, NY 13420
   (315) 369-3838
   www.webbhistory.org

The Goodsell Museum features six rooms of continually changing exhibits, artifacts, photographs, and memorabilia of early life in the Adirondacks.

7. Great Camp Sagamore
   Sagamore Road, Raquette Lake, NY 13436
   (315) 354-5311
   www.sagamore.org

For more than fifty years, Sagamore served as the summer retreat of the Alfred G. Vanderbilt family. Today Sagamore is the only Great Camp operating as a nonprofit organization. It is open to the public for tours.

8. Jane McCrea's Grave

Union Cemetery, 8 Schuyler Street, Hudson Falls, NY 12828

Union Cemetery opened for burials in 1847. It was officially named "The Sandy Hill and Fort Edward Union Cemetery" and is the primary burying ground for the villages of Hudson Falls and Fort Edward. It contains the well-known gravesites of Jane McCrea, murdered in 1777, and Duncan Campbell of the Black Watch.

9. Lake George Battlefield Park

Fort George Road (office is 139 Beach Road, Lake George, NY 12845)

(518) 668-3352

This thirty-five-acre park was the setting for the battle of Lake George in 1755. Historic monuments include a statue of Father Isaac Jogues, the first European man to have seen Lake George; a bronze sculpture of a Native American; a monument dedicated to General William Johnson and King Hendrick of the Mohawks. This also contains the remains of the southwest bastion of Fort George, commenced in 1759.

10. Lake George Historical Association

290 Canada Street, Lake George, NY 12845

(518) 668-5044

The Lake George Historical Association (LGHA) is a not-for-profit organization dedicated to the preservation of the history of the Lake George region. Located in the Historic Warren County Court House at Canada and Amherst Streets in Lake George Village, this 1845 brick structure is home for the Lake George Historical Association and its collection of artifacts.

11. North Star Underground Railroad Museum in Keeseville

634 Route 373, Keeseville, NY 12944

(518) 834-9990

The Underground Railroad helped tens of thousands of slaves escape to freedom before the Civil War, and thousands came through the Lake Champlain corridor to Canada. This museum brings to life that struggle for freedom as it played out in the Lake Champlain / Adirondack region.

12. Penfield Homestead Museum
   703 Creek Road, Crown Point, NY 12928
   (518) 597-3804
   www.penfieldmuseum.org

The central feature of Penfield Homestead Museum is the ca. 1825 Penfield Homestead, which features first-floor rooms that depict early nineteenth-century life, including a formal parlor, mining business office, main kitchen, and summer kitchen. The first floor also features displays on Crown Point history. The second floor includes three bedrooms, a clothing and toy room, and a hallway and room dedicated to Crown Point's involvement in the Civil War. A replica of Joseph Henry's electro-magnet is the highlight of the wood-shed tour. It was the partnership between Allen Penfield, original builder of this homestead and iron industry pioneer, and Joseph Henry, inventor of the electro-magnet and first secretary of the Smithsonian, that gave rise to "the Birthplace of the Electrical Age." The museum also boasts two walking trails, one of which is a walk back in time through the Crown Point Iron Company manufacturing complex.

13. The Wild Center
   45 Museum Drive, Tupper Lake, NY 12986
   (518) 359-7800
   www.wildcenter.org

The Wild Center is a natural history center at Tupper Lake, near the center of the Adirondack Park. There are five primary indoor exhibit areas on the eighty-one-acre campus. The center features live exhibits and live animals, including river otters, birds, amphibians, and fish.

FURTHER READING

Abel, Timothy J. 2015a. "Finding Cantonment Saranac: The Search for Col. Zebulon Pike's 1812–1813 Winter Cantonment in Plattsburgh, New York." *Northeast Historical Archaeology* 44:147–161.

———. 2015b. "Storrs Harbor: Archaeology of a War of 1812 Naval Shipyard on Lake Ontario." *Bulletin, Journal of the New York State Archaeological Association* 129:19–35.

———. 2016. "'I Wish You Could See the Style in Which We Live': Archaeology of a Soldier's Cabin at Cantonment Saranac, Plattsburgh, New York." In *Archaeology of the War of 1812*, edited by Michael T. Lucas and Julie M. Schablitsky, 57–74. New York: Routledge.

Adamson, Lisa, ed. 2017. *Native American Presence, Lake George: Ancestral Lands and Voices, Lost, Reclaimed*. Lake George Historical Association.

Allen, Ross F., James C. Dawson, Morris F. Glenn, Robert B. Gordon, David J. Killick, and Richard W. Ward. 1990. "An Archeological Survey of Bloomery Forges in the Adirondacks." *IA, the Journal of the Society for Industrial Archeology* 16(1): 3–20.

Baker, Brenda J., and Christina B. Rieth. 2000. "Beyond the Massacre: Historic and Prehistoric Activity at Fort William Henry." *Northeast Anthropology* 60:45–61.

Barlow, Ronald S. 1992. *The Vanishing American Outhouse*. El Cajon, CA: Windmill.

Bellico, Russell P. 1992. *Sails and Steam in the Mountains — a Maritime and Military History of Lake George and Lake Champlain*. Fleischmanns, NY: Purple Mountain.

———. 1995. *Chronicles of Lake George: Journeys in War and Peace*. Fleischmanns, NY: Purple Mountain.

———. 2010. *Empires in the Mountains: French and Indian War Campaigns and Forts in the Lake Champlain, Lake George, and Hudson River Corridor*. Fleischmanns, NY: Purple Mountain.

Benes, Peter, ed. 1988. *The Farm*. Dublin Seminar for New England Folklife Annual Proceedings 1986. Trustees of Boston University.

"Bike Tourism Should Pedal Forward." 2017. Editorial in *Glens Falls Post-Star*, March 9, A6.

Blackwell, Jon. 1996. "Late Recognition: Exhuming of Bodies at Fort William Henry Sheds Light on Black Soldiers' Contribution in French and Indian War." *Schenectady Sunday Gazette*, December 1, 1996.

Bramen, Lisa. 2016. "Abandoned Adirondacks: Finding Beauty in Decay." *Adirondack Life*, October, 52–55, 65.

———. 2017. "From Ore to Orchids: The Legacy of Benson Mines." *Adirondack Life*, January/February, 34–39, 69.

Calver, William Louis, and Reginald Pelham Bolton. 1950. *History Written with Pick and Shovel*. New York: New-York Historical Society.

Campbell, J. Duncan. 1958. "Investigations at the French Village, Fort Ticonderoga, NY." *Bulletin of the Fort Ticonderoga Museum* 9(2): 143–155.

Carl, James D. 2009. "Mining in the Adirondack Mountains — Three Examples." In *Inside the Blue Line: Essays on Adirondack Environments*, edited by Anthony O. Tyler and Michael Wilson, 72–128. Potsdam, NY: SUNY Potsdam Press.

Coffin, Howard, Will Curtis, and Jane Curtis. 2005. *Guns over the Champlain Valley: A Guide to Historic Military Sites and Battlefields*. Woodstock, VT: Countryman.

Collamer & Associates. 2003. Phase IB & Phase II/III Cultural Resource Investigations for the Quaker Road Retail Development (96PR3046). Bay and Quaker Roads, Town of Queensbury, Warren County, NY.

Cooper, James Fenimore. (1826) 1980. *The Last of the Mohicans*. New York: Reprint, Penguin Books.

Crisman, Kevin J. 1986. *Of Sailing Ships and Sidewheelers: The History and Nautical Archaeology of Lake Champlain*. Montpelier: Division for Historic Preservation, Agency of Development and Community Affairs, State of Vermont.

Crisman, Kevin J., and Arthur B. Cohn. 1994. "Lake Champlain Nautical Archaeology since 1980." *Journal of Vermont Archaeology* 1:153–166.

Davis, Jeremy K. 2012. *Lost Ski Areas of the Southern Adirondacks*. Charleston, SC: History Press.

———. 2014. *Lost Ski Areas of the Northern Adirondacks*. Charleston, SC: History Press.

Donaldson, Alfred L. 1996. *A History of the Adirondacks*. 2 vols. Fleischmanns, NY: Purple Mountain. Originally published in 1921.

Dunn, Shirley W. 1994. *The Mohicans and Their Land, 1609–1730*. Fleischmanns, NY: Purple Mountain.

Esch, Mary. 2012. "Group Restores Old Town." *Glens Falls Post-Star*, July 16, A1, A6.

———. 2016. "Chasing Down Answers." *Glens Falls Post-Star*, April 25, A1, A5.

Feister, Lois M. 1984a. "Building Material Indicative of Status Differentiation at the Crown Point Barracks." *Historical Archaeology* 18(1): 103–107.

———. 1984b. "Material Culture of the British Soldier at 'His Majesty's Fort of Crown Point' on Lake Champlain, New York, 1759–1783." *Journal of Field Archaeology* 11(2): 123–132.

Feister, Lois M., and Paul R. Huey. 1985. "Archaeological Testing at Fort Gage, a Provincial Redoubt of 1758 at Lake George, New York." *Bulletin and Journal of Archaeology for New York State* 90:49–59.

Fisher, Charles L. 1995. "The Archaeology of Provincial Officers' Huts at Crown Point State Historic Site." *Northeast Historical Archaeology* 24:65–86.

Folwell, Elizabeth. 1992. *The Adirondack Book: A Complete Guide*. Stockbridge, MA: Berkshire House.

Fox, William F. 1901. *History of the Lumber Industry in the State of New York*. Harrison, NY: Harbor Hill Books.

Funk, Robert E. 1976. Recent Contributions to Hudson Valley Prehistory. *New York State Museum Memoir* no. 22. Albany: New York State Museum.

Gereau, Leonard A. 2014. *Tahawus Memories, 1941–1963: The Story of a Unique Adirondack Hometown*. Saranac Lake, NY: Hungry Bear.

Gifford, Stanley M. 1955. *Fort Wm. Henry — a History*. Lake George, NY: Fort William Henry.

Gilborn, Craig. 2000. *Adirondack Camps: Homes Away from Home, 1850–1950*. Adirondack Museum / Syracuse University Press.

Godine, Amy. 1998. "Friends and Neighbors: Tracing Quaker Roots in the North Country." *Adirondack Life,* May/June, 58–65.

Gruse, Doug. 2014. "Cultural Wasteland: Privies and Dumps Hold Historical Clues." *Glens Falls Post-Star,* May 5, A1, A6.

Hagerty, Meg. 2014. "Storytown Saga." *Glens Falls Post-Star,* August 21, A1, A5.

Hall, Russell J. 2005. *Gem of the Adirondacks: Star Lake, Benson Mines, and the Global Economy.* Gainesville, FL: Lighthall Books.

Hart, John P., and Christina B. Rieth, eds. 2002. "Northeast Subsistence-Settlement Change, A.D. 700–1300." *New York State Museum Bulletin* 496. Albany.

Hartgen Archeological Associates. 1985. Adirondack Park Archeological Site Inventory Update. Troy, NY. Unpublished report.

Hill, William H. 1928. *Old Fort Edward before 1800.* Privately printed.

Hochschild, Harold K. 1962a. *Adirondack Railroads: Real and Phantom.* Blue Mountain Lake, NY: Adirondack Museum.

———. 1962b. *Lumberjacks and Rivermen in the Central Adirondacks, 1850–1950.* Blue Mountain Lake, NY: Adirondack Museum.

———. 1962c. *The MacIntyre Mine — from Failure to Fortune.* Blue Mountain Lake, NY: Adirondack Museum.

Hodges, Richard. 2016. "The Adirondacks: Vacationing in the Wild." *Current World Archaeology* 74:48–51.

Johnson, Arthur L. 2009. "Not Quite a Century: The Railroad Era in the Adirondacks." In *Inside the Blue Line: Essays on Adirondack Environments,* edited by Anthony O. Tyler and Michael Wilson, 50–71. Potsdam, NY: SUNY Potsdam Press.

Johnson, Dennis. 1993. "Romancing the Stone: How Barton Mines Became the Most Abrasive Company in the World." *Adirondack Life,* March/April, 46–51, 57.

Kaiser, Harvey H. 1982. *Great Camps of the Adirondacks.* Boston: David R. Godine.

Keller, Jane Eblen. 1980. *Adirondack Wilderness: A Story of Man and Nature.* Syracuse, NY: Syracuse University Press.

Kilroy, Roger. 1996. *The Compleat Loo: A Lavatorial Miscellany.* New York: Barnes & Noble Books.

Kochan, James L., ed. 1993. "Joseph Frye's Journal and Map of the Siege of Fort William Henry, 1757." *Bulletin of the Fort Ticonderoga Museum* 15(5): 339–61.

Kourofsky, Niki. 2009. "What Lies Beneath: Archaeologists Dust off a 50-Year-Old Crown Point Mystery." *Adirondack Life,* May/June, 58–61.

Kravic, Frank J. 1971. "Colonial Crown Point and Its Artifacts." *Northeast Historical Archaeology* 1(1): 20–21.

Krueger, John W., Arthur B. Cohn, Kevin J. Crisman, Heidi Miksch, and Jane M. Lape. 1985. *The Bulletin of the Fort Ticonderoga Museum* 14(6). Thematic issue devoted to the Fort Ticonderoga King's Shipyard excavation.

Kudish, Michael. 1985. *Where Did the Tracks Go: Following Railroad Grades in the Adirondacks.* Saranac Lake, NY: Chauncy Press.

———. 1996. *Railroads of the Adirondacks: A History.* Fleischmanns, NY: Purple Mountain.

Lehman, Don. 2013a. "Lake George Project Halted." *Glens Falls Post-Star,* October 25, A1, A5.

———. 2013b. "Past Uncovered at Dig." *Glens Falls Post-Star,* November 1, A1, A6.

———. 2014. "Students Observe History." *Glens Falls Post-Star,* May 10, B1, B8.

Liston, Maria A., and Brenda J. Baker. 1995. "Reconstructing the Massacre at Fort William Henry, New York." *International Journal of Osteoarchaeology* 6:28–41.

Longstreth, Richard. 2017. *A Guide to Architecture in the Adirondacks*. Keeseville, NY: Adirondack Architectural Heritage.

Lucas, Michael T., and Julie M. Schablitsky, eds. 2016. *Archaeology of the War of 1812*. New York: Routledge.

Manchester, Lee, ed. 2007. *Tales from the Deserted Village: First-Hand Accounts of Early Explorations into the Heart of the Adirondacks*. Privately published.

Masten, Arthur H. 1968. *The Story of Adirondac*. Syracuse, NY: Syracuse University Press.

McMartin, Barbara. 1891. *Hides, Hemlocks and Adirondack History: How the Tanning Industry Influenced the Region's Growth*. Utica, NY: North Country Books.

Namias, June. 1993. *White Captives: Gender and Ethnicity on the American Frontier*. Chapel Hill, NC: University of North Carolina Press.

Northeast Historical Archaeology. 2001–2002. Special Issue: Historic Preservation and the Archaeology of Nineteenth-Century Farmsteads in the Northeast. Edited by Sherene Baugher and Terry H. Klein. Vols. 30–31.

———. 2015. Special Issue: War of 1812. Edited by Susan E. Maguire. Vol. 44.

Open Space Institute. 2009. "Tahawus Historic Core Area Master Plan." Newcomb, NY. Prepared by Sasaki Associates Inc. for the Open Space Institute.

The Original People: Native Americans in the Champlain Valley. 1988. Museum catalog based on an exhibition at the Clinton County Historical Museum, City Hall, Plattsburgh, NY, June 10–November 29, 1988.

Parker, Arthur C. 1922. "The Archeological History of New York, Part 1 and Part 2." *New York State Museum Bulletin*, nos. 235, 236. Albany: University of the State of New York.

Podskoch, Martin. 2011. *Adirondack Civilian Conservation Corps Camps*. East Hampton, CT: Podskoch Press.

Pollard, Gordon C., and Haagen D. Klaus. 2004. "A Large Business: The Clintonville Site, Resources, and Scale at Adirondack Bloomery Forges." *IA, the Journal of the Society for Industrial Archeology* 30(1): 19–46.

Pope, Connie. n.d. "Hammondville: Essex County Ghost Town." Unpublished manuscript. www.knobpond.com/HammondvilleHistory/Essex county ghost town.pdf.

Quiggle, Robert, and Matthew Kirk. 2015. "Industrial Progress in the Adirondacks: The Archaeological Evidence of the Transition from Extractive Enterprises to Renewable Energy." *Northeast Anthropology* 83/84:185–212.

Rathje, William L. 1974. "The Garbage Project: A New Way of Looking at the Problems of Archaeology." *Archaeology* 27:236–241.

Rathje, William L., and Cullen Murphy. 2001. *Rubbish! The Archaeology of Garbage*. Tucson: University of Arizona Press.

Ritchie, William A. 1969. *The Archaeology of New York State*. Rev. ed. Garden City, NY: Natural History Press.

Roberts, Jesse David. 1961. *Bears, Bibles, and a Boy: Memories of the Adirondacks*. New York: W. W. Norton.

Rolando, Victor. 1992. *200 Years of Soot and Sweat: The History and Archeology of Vermont's Iron, Charcoal, and Lime Industries*. Manchester Center, VT: Mountain Publications and the Vermont Archaeological Society.

Ross, Wilford C. 1976. *The History of Graphite, New York*. Glens Falls, NY: Ridgecraft Books.

Seely, Bruce E. 1981. "Blast Furnace Technology in the Mid-19th Century: A Case Study of the Adirondack Iron and Steel Company." *IA, the Journal of the Society for Industrial Archeology* 7:27–54.

Snow, Dean R. 1977. "The Archaic of the Lake George Region." In *Amerinds and Their Paleoenvironments in Northeastern North America*, edited by Walter Newman and Bert Salwen. *Annals of the New York Academy of Sciences* 288:431–438.

———. 1980. *The Archaeology of New England*. New York: Academic.

———. 1996. *In Mohawk Country: Early Narratives of a Native People*. Syracuse, NY: Syracuse University Press.

Stager, Curt. 2017. "Hidden Heritage." *Adirondack Life*, May/June, 54–66.

Staley, David P. 2012. "'I Trust There Will Be No Failure . . .': The Importance of Bricks and Brickmaking at the Adirondack Iron and Steel Company's Upper Works." *IA, the Journal of the Society for Industrial Archeology* 38(1): 4–26.

———. 2016. "Last Gasp: The Construction, Operation, and Dissolution of the Adirondack Iron and Steel Company's 'New Furnace.'" *Northeast Historical Archaeology* 45:171–199.

Starbuck, David R. 1990. "A Retrospective on Archaeology at Fort William Henry, 1952–1993: Retelling the Tale of *The Last of the Mohicans*." *Northeast Historical Archaeology* 20:8–26.

———. 1993. "Anatomy of a Massacre." *Archaeology* 46 (November/December): 42–46.

———. 1998. "The Big Dig: Looking for Traces of Fort William Henry's Brutal Past." *Adirondack Life*, September/October, 44–49, 77–78.

———. 1999. *The Great Warpath: British Military Sites from Albany to Crown Point*. Hanover, NH: University Press of New England.

———. 2000. "History Homework." *Adirondack Life*, July/August, 62–65, 99–100.

———. 2001. "Beneath the Bubblegum." *Archaeology* 54 (January/February): 22–23.

———. 2002a. "Hallowed Ground: Exploring Lake George Battlefield Park." *Adirondack Life*, Annual Guide, 14–22.

———. 2002b. *Massacre at Fort William Henry*. Hanover, NH: University Press of New England.

———. 2004a. *Rangers and Redcoats on the Hudson*. Hanover, NH: University Press of New England.

———. 2004b. "The Scientific Investigation of Jane McCrea." *Journal of the Washington County Historical Society*, 4–23.

———. 2006a. "Fort Edward Martyr Mystery." *Adirondack Life*, November/December, 50–53, 62.

———. 2006b. "The Mystery of the Second Body." *Plymouth Magazine*, Winter, 14–15.

———. 2008. "The 'Massacre' at Fort William Henry: History, Archaeology, and Reenactment." *Expedition* 50:17–25.

———. 2009. "The Starbuck Farm: How an Archaeologist Started to Dig His Roots." *Adirondack Life*, Collectors Issue 2009, 70–74.

———. 2010. *Excavating the Sutlers' House: Artifacts of the British Armies in Fort Edward and Lake George*. Hanover, NH: University Press of New England.

———. 2011. *The Archaeology of Forts and Battlefields*. Gainesville: University Press of Florida.

———. 2014. *The Legacy of Fort William Henry*. Hanover, NH: University Press of New England.

Stoltie, Annie. 2016. "High Profile: Our Enduring Fascination with Adirondack Fire Towers." *Adirondack Life*, October, 42–51.

Sulavik, Stephen B. 2005. *Adirondack: Of Indians and Mountains, 1535–1838*. Fleischmanns, NY: Purple Mountain.

Todish, Timothy J. 2002. *The Annotated and Illustrated Journals of Major Robert Rogers*. Fleischmanns, NY: Purple Mountain.

Tolles, Bryant F., Jr. 2003. *Resort Hotels of the Adirondacks: The Architecture of a Summer Paradise, 1850–1950*. Hanover, NH: University Press of New England.

Toscano, Bill. 2013. "Dig through the Dump." *Glens Falls Post-Star*, June 17, A1, A6.

Tyler, Anthony O., and Michael Wilson, eds. 2009. *Inside the Blue Line: Essays on Adirondack Environments*. Potsdam, NY: SUNY Potsdam Press.

Verner, William K. 1968. *The Story of Adirondac*. Adirondack Museum/Syracuse University Press. First edition privately printed, 1923.

Weatherwax, Carolyn O. 2008. "Graphite Products Corporation: Graphite Mining/Processing Operation; Wilton/Greenfield, New York." *SIA New England Chapters Newsletter* 29(2): 12–17.

Weinman, Tom. 2017. "Discovery and Excavations at Two Key Lake George, NY, Prehistoric Sites." Paper presented at the annual meeting of the New York State Archaeological Association, Lake George, NY, April 22, 2017.

Williams, Donald R. 2002. *The Adirondacks, 1830–1930*. Charleston, SC: Arcadia.

Wilson, David. 1853. *The Life of Jane McCrea, with an Account of Burgoyne's Expedition in 1777*. Toronto: Toronto Public Library.

Wiseman, Frederick Matthew. 2001. *The Voice of the Dawn: An Autohistory of the Abenaki Nation*. Hanover, NH: University Press of New England.

Wolff, Phil. 2010. "Knowing Noah John." *Adirondack Life*, May/June, 32–37.

Woods, Lynn. 1994. "A History in Fragments." *Adirondack Life*, November/December, 30–37, 61, 68–71, 78–79.

Yamin, Rebecca, et al. 2000. *Tales of Five Points: Working-Class Life in Nineteenth-Century New York*. 7 vols. Washington, DC: U.S. General Services Administration.

Zaboly, Gary Stephen. 2004. *A True Ranger: The Life and Many Wars of Major Robert Rogers*. Garden City Park, NY: Royal Blockhouse.

Zarzynski, Joseph W., and Bob Benway. 2011. *Lake George Shipwrecks and Sunken History*. Charleston, SC: History Press.

INDEX

Note: Page numbers in **bold** refer to illustrations.